AFTER THE LINE

GREAT LAKES BOOKS

AFTER THE LINE

JOSIE KEARNS

WAYNE STATE UNIVERSITY PRESS   DETROIT

94 93 92 91 90   5 4 3 2 1

Library of Congress Cataloging-in-Publication Data

Kearns, Josie, 1954–
 Life after the line / Josie Kearns.
  p.   cm.—(Great Lakes books)
  ISBN 0-8143-2015-5 (alk. paper).—ISBN 0-8143-2016-3 (pbk. :
alk. paper)
  1. Automobile industry workers—United States—Interviews.
2. Unemployed—United States—Interviews. I. Title. II. Series.
HD8039.A82U647   1990
331.13'78292'0973—dc20   90-11936
                                                     CIP

This book is dedicated to my husband, Joseph Matuzak, of course, for his inspiration and wonderful nagging. To my mother, Gladys Randall Luchenbill, the better storyteller. My mother-in-law, Mary Matuzak, for her conversations. To Ken Hannon and Valerie Clarke, for their help. To the Torch Bar, for its indulgence and atmosphere. To each person in this book, who freely gave me their time and experience. To the people of Flint. And to Mr. Cat, posthumously.

Special thanks to Mary Ann Chick Whiteside and the *Flint Journal* for giving me a chance.

Contents

Introduction

This is not a book of theories, although many are proposed by those interviewed. Nor is it about politics or economics, nor a handbook on the United Auto Workers Union and General Motors Corporation, though opinions abound on all.

It is about people and what happens to them in transition, namely, the transition from being an autoworker in General Motors plants in Flint, Michigan, to being unemployed, and sometimes—through training or determination—to being in another career. This is a shoe's eye view by the people who are most affected. A view which often reflects incredible resilience in the face of adversity as well as obstinancy, true bravery and hope amid despair, a willingness and a push toward change as well as the rigidity to hold onto the comforting status quo.

Also, this is a book of perspectives. I did not set out to present one opinion or uphold one conviction. It is probably possible to line up twenty people in agreement to present a single facet of life after the line. Here, however, people disagree directly with each other, while others echo a resonance. This is a book of many voices because I talked to a diverse population. There is no one die cast of "autoworker" or "laborer." These people are entrepreneurs, hobbyists, writers, builders, college students, environmentalists, electricians, managers, and yoga experts.

One of the comforting surprises about these extensive interviews is that, although not a statistical sampling, they accurately reflect findings by other institutions, centers, and training programs. In talking to David Rhodes, a job developer at the UAW–GM Human Resource Center, whose interview appears in this book, it is clear that the idea of shoveling people into massive training programs and shoveling them out to waiting jobs does not exactly work. Sometimes half of the people in a program drop out, while others may finish training only to find a job in an unrelated field. The concept of treating the individual and developing a lifelong career plan, not a spot check, seems more realistic. Asking "What do you want to do?"; and then pairing that with needed or already learned skills works best. This is, as

Rhodes says, "treating people as a natural resource as important as the Great Lakes."

I have spoken with a number of workers in nontraditional occupations, which is more the norm than the exception, as reflected by findings of the New Work Center at the University of Michigan–Flint, directed by Dr. Fritjof Bergman and Dr. Richard Gull. Both agree that the twin loss of identity and livelihood is also emotional and not to be dealt with lightly.

They also point to hope for a new order of worklife. Through a number of grants and with the help of WFUM Channel 28, they have produced a series of public television interviews and a program which helps high school students take a new, long-term look at the work they wish to do.

As plants close, many financial and psychological hardships are certain. But there also may be some positive effects. Never again will high school students be able to "just go into the shop and disappear." They will have to learn something—a base of skills to apply to the growing competition in the job market. Even now, high school counselors prepare Career Days specifically designed to inform students of options and training needed for designated fields.

Or, as Dr. Bergman says, "Is it ever good to think that you can lift a door handle eight to ten hours for the rest of your life?" His words parallel Plato's statement that "an unexamined life is not worth living."

In gathering information it was my fortune to first describe the culture of autoworkers, and later discover that my investigation mirrored others' forays into this culture. Culture is an accurate term, for these people, with all their individuality, express a culture that has its own symbols, rewards, punishments, aspirations, theory, and, yes, language.

It is a language of terms like Paragraph 96, SUB-pay, TAPP, high pay, low pay, national contract, job banks, and New Concept; and of mechanical names like Foxtail, R and Bs, rivets, and Excello; but it is a language all the same.

Except for a few instances, my method was to interview each person extensively, often for hours. Some people were interviewed more than once. The interviews were transcribed and then edited for clarification. The "uhs, ums" have been excised, as have repetitions and unrelated material. Wherever possible, my questions have been deleted. Often when a topic resurfaced in an interview, quotes on the same topic have been compressed into one point in this transcription. My purpose in doing all of this was to make the material more readable and the speaker succinct.

Some of the terms in this book are explained below.

Paragraph 96. This is the famous paragraph, drafted into the UAW's national contract, which allowed workers laid off at one plant to flow into other GM plants and carry with them intact seniority. Thus, although the Buick and AC plants themselves did not close, workers at those places with less seniority than workers coming from the closed Fisher plant could be and were laid off as the result of a closing.

Many workers did not take this option, thinking that their plant would not close or that they would eventually be called back. This option is also responsible for "pitting one worker against another" in a competition for existing jobs, as Corleen Proulx of Local 599 states.

SUB-pay (Supplemental Unemployment Benefits). Originally, SUB-pay benefits, checks totalling near the amount a worker would normally be paid, were in terms of fifty-two credits or higher, depending upon seniority. Thus, at the rate of one credit per week, some workers had a cushion of a whole year or more before touching unemployment benefits. The money was gathered through the efforts of the UAW.

Unfortunately, SUB-pay was determined on a proportional formula. And, as more were laid off, the rate of credits increased from one credit per week to several. Thus, the time off at the same rate of pay shrunk from two or one year to six months and is still shrinking as plants close.

Job bank. According to a story in the *Detroit Free Press,* (Monday, February 1, 1987, page 1C), this program was won by the UAW in 1984 and reinforced in contract bargaining in 1987. Workers in the job bank may receive full pay for months or years and although laid off are "on call" to GM and often tend vegetable gardens, work in youth programs, or do other small tasks. Cindy Carson, an assembly worker at General Motors Delco Remy factory in Anderson, Indiana, completed a four-year degree in journalism while in the job bank and now reports for the *Muncie Star,* an Indiana daily.

However, in Flint, workers in job banks remain on call.

GIS. Guaranteed Income Stream benefits guaranteed that a certain amount of money was coming to laid-off workers.

TAPP Funds. Tuition Assistance Pay Program was also a UAW-negotiated benefit. It provided up to $5,500 per year to those working for educational courses. When laid off, $5,500 was the total for education and training. However, if a worker was called back and then laid off again, the $5,500 figure began anew. Thus, about ten percent of workers had some sort of education and/or training when laid off, according to David Rhodes.

Golden Handshake. This is the so-called buy-out offered by GM to many long-term employees. It is a lump sum in amounts ranging from $30,000 to $55,000, depending upon taxes and other considerations, such as length of service. Many workers with ten years or more seniority have already taken the buy-out and begun new lives. In offering the buy-out, GM dissolves all responsibilities to that employee, including insurance benefits and tuition refunds, SUB-funds, and any benefits negotiated through the UAW contract.

And some philosophy follows.

What is philosophy, if not what one lives by? The ten- and fifteen- and twenty-year workers have definitely lived by a system. And they tell you about it.

I've tried to focus on those who have made, or are in the process of making, a successful transition to a new lifestyle. Those who have found an answer to the question *What next?* Thus, this is not a representative sampling. Of the over eight thousand (and counting) laid off, many have not made that final transition to a new source of income, even thought about it seriously. In the face of several plant closings and predicted line lay-offs, many wait to be called back.

So this is not so much a book of answers but a book of possibilities. These are the stories of how some people made decisions about what work they eventually wanted to do. They tell you how they got through, what worked for them and what didn't, how they got over the shock or didn't, how they failed and how they succeeded.

I only hope I've been able to be true to their words, to reflect their thoughts and stories as accurately as they generously told them to me. But the stories revolve around an old question: *What do you do with people?* I think most have creatively answered that and may show the way for others to go. Or at least how to begin.

There are also questions of responsibility.

What makes one person able to accept and grow with change? What makes an entrepreneur? What should the union, what should GM, have done and when? Why can some people dive into something completely new and others not? Are women hit the worst in a layoff? Minorities? What helps people make the adjustment to a new career?

I have not found all of the answers, but I offer some of the stories.

PART 1

THE DAY FISHER 1 CLOSED

General Motors Fisher Body Plant, Fisher 1 or Fisher, as it was commonly called closed December 10, 1987, at about 2:30 P.M. It was the site of the famous 1937 sit-down strike that marked the beginnings of the UAW and workers' rights. Although historical markers had been placed on its sides heralding the battles won in 1937, fifty years later some felt they had lost the war.

Hand-made signs that hung out the shop windows said, "Here today, gone tomorrow. Fisher 1," and, "1937 sit down— 1987 shut down." Everyone seemed to be aware of the historical irony; this Flint, Michigan, plant, the birthplace of so much hope, was closing down.

The so-called "ripple effect" was felt dramatically by two bars in operation just across the street from Fisher. One was Ethel's Bar, whose owner of twenty-six years had already decided to close its doors forever the following week, realizing the bars' dependence on shop trade. The other, the Korner Bar, was owned by a former shop worker who had quit Fisher seven years earlier to enjoy a second career as a bar owner. In a curious "double whammy," the shop now, for the second time, would play a major part in this man's livelihood as he faced the loss of clientele, the autoworkers once employed by Fisher.

The following comments were recorded on that day, strangely calm yet sad, when thirty-six hundred workers, many with a decade or more of service, would see their fellows for the last time.

This is an introduction to complicated issues spoken in clear language by the people most affected. There is a kind of whirlwind surrounding them that will change their lives forever. And in it blow questions of rights, responsibility, and change.

1

On the Sidewalk Outside the Plant

Everything seems gray in the semi-cold. A lot of people who don't seem to belong are here with flashy equipment hung over tweed hats and long wool coats—photographers and reporters. There are at least four camera crews: Keva Productions; WDIV Channel 4 from Detroit; WJRT Channel 12 at a side gate; and former editor of the Michigan Voice *and ex-writer from* Mother Jones, *activist Michael Moore, who is making a film about plant closings. People who do belong are in Local 599 silk jackets, in blue jeans and industrial work clothes. The small clumps of people mill around as if they are part of a moving company waiting for something to break. But the overcast sky is impenetrable.*

Anonymous Woman

How long did you work for Buick?

Eleven years.

And you're out here supporting workers?

Right. Right. Well, it's all workers. That's what we wanted to do, get it into the mind of workers that it is not Fisher Body workers' fault that we're losing our jobs. They didn't make those decisions. It's inept union leadership that didn't fight for anything, like they didn't fight two years ago about the closing. They didn't fight our shift layoff in August when it was announced. Didn't fight it and we're fighting the management.

Do you think that this has anything to do with, that the plant they're shutting down is . . .

. . . is historic, where the sit-down strike was and it's great revenge, I think. I think it's from the company. Sure, sure.

If you look, when was the last time that you knew that anybody fought what was happening. You know? We workers, I mean they organized the UAW to represent workers' interests. And now we hear from Beiber, who is president of the international, "But we have to be partners with General Motors."

And a contract that he's telling us is job security and in the same breath saying it's okay for General Motors to shut down sixteen plants, get rid of thirty-six hundred people, that they don't matter. Now that's the kind of leadership we've got. And people have sat back and we've listened and believed what they've told us for the last thirty some years.

And it's nothing.

You put this down, no matter what. The workers have to reorganize as workers and to be true solidarity. We don't have solidarity. Not when International makes decisions that knows they're going to put workers from Fisher Body in positions of animosity at other plants. And it's happening all over.

We have no leadership.

You mean it's like everybody's fighting everybody for the jobs?

Well that is what—that's the position we're all put into.

I believe union officials did not want to have a vigil and it wasn't all union officials, it was shop committee. You talk to Mike Palmer and standing committees, they said it was good, okay.

Do they ask the members? You know? Any decision they make they're not asking the members. But they didn't want to create anything where they would have to answer to the workers. You know.

Emerson Shawl

I took an early retirement, mutual agreement, because I was in disagreement with policy, disagreement with the union, disagreement with many things happening in the plant.

So you're out here to show support?

My father was an original sit-downer here.

Bill Perkins

Were you here at the original sit-down strike?

Yes I was here inside, yup.

Was it very scary to be in there at that time?

No, they fed us pretty good. (Laughs.)
    I was young, that was a fun time in my life. We weren't in prison here.

Why are you here today?

Cause it's the last day. And I'm seventy-eight.

Ray Lord

I was the first vice president of Chevrolet local for about ten years.

Why are you out here today then?

Well I'm out here today because this is really a sad event for Flint and I . . . I'm just surprised. They're treating it like it was a hot dog stand closing.
    You know, I know politicians worked these plant gates for fifty years with their literature. I don't see one politician out here today and that's disgraceful.
    You know, not long ago we put a historical marker here and the politicians almost crowded us out. But now I don't see any of them. And that's a shame. Shame on them.

What do you do now?

I'm retired out of the plant.

Are you seeing a lot of friends come out of those doors?

I haven't yet. But you know, a lot of the active union guys were transferred over to Buick local, I'm sure you know that. So . . . but I'm just amazed that there's not many people here.

What interests me is that it's the site of the sit-down strike. Do you have any feelings about that?

That's what makes it so sad. Whether it's intentional or not, who knows? I know they're in business to make money, so. I don't think they would lose any money just for that reason. But that's what makes it so sad.

You know there was a worldwide industrial revolution because of what happened right here. And you see, that's what's got me upset. Really.

James Holden

Today is your last day?

Well, no the 18th. I have twenty-two years. I'm a skilled trades painter.

Why are you down here today?

I worked today, but I came out with this Jobs and Justice group to kind of give support to some of the people that's getting laid off that won't have a job. Some of the people will go to Buick. I don't know about myself. I'm not even sure about my . . . my job future.

Do you have any other job plans?

Well, I'll be out trying to . . . beating the bushes trying to find other work for myself, plus I put into the area-wide pool. But I will continue to work with the Jobs and Justice group to try to, you know, enhance a group that might talk to them.

What they're advocating is the fact that we need to talk to one of the political systems to try and stop some of this outsourcing that the plants might be closed.

Do you have friends that are being laid off today?

Quite a few. It's kind of a sad situation. You didn't get inside the plant, did you?

No.

Well, there's not a lot of happy faces in there. Some of the older guys that have enough time to retire feel just as much at home here as they do in their own homes. And then some of the younger people that came in expecting a future out of it—they, they're pretty devastated.

In fact, some of them have made idle threats and you know, different sorts of things that upset people, you know?

Have you heard what anybody's going to do afterward?

You know, we have quite a few people who will take that Golden Handshake. So, some are going that way and others are going the direction of relocating, some that are older and have more than ten years. It's all different directions.

But the people who don't have enough time [in] to go anywhere, yeah, those people are pretty devastated. They have no ideas of what the future's going to be about. Some of the ones that did have lower seniority are trying to take the Golden Handshake. Applying for it.

But I'm sure that they are only going to give out so many. And then that's it.

It's a lot of money.

Well it don't make no difference to General Motors, they gave away $700 million didn't they? It don't make no difference.

This is a historical site and it's in my mind that General Motors . . . the workers made such commotion about the sit-down strike so it's fifty years, put up all these plaques. So I think that had a little impact on shutting it down. I'm sure that they could renovate it and renew the paint systems, punching, you know, keep this plant open.

It would be cheaper to renovate it than to build a new plant.

Their idea is to get a big tax break, write this place off and maybe sell it. They're trying to sell it now.

Yes, there's other things that can be produced here.

What do you think about their commitment to the workers?

You take people like Roger Smith that's already got millions of dollars, they don't even think about the poor people that's out here starving to death, the street people and all that. They could care less. They might give a donation.

Originally, back when they had the press room and all that going we had around eight thousand people here. Then they first, in '83 they shut the press room down. We went down to about five-thousand. Then they shut the south unit down, we went down to three thousand.

Do you think people are prepared because they had some time to think about the shutdown?

Some of the people are really giving up. I mean they've just given up the idea of continuing in General Motors and some of them are looking to maybe other sources of jobs, maybe taking a certain amount of school.

But see, it's not only happening with General Motors. It's happening all over the country with all the corporations. That's what the Jobs and Justice is about. What good is it going to do to get a quality education when there is no jobs out there to apply that to?

You know, it'll be a handful, a few people.

For instance, like I said once we had eight thousand people here running this plant. They could start up the same production and probably have half that amount of people running it. Now. So this is what the corporations are headed for. That's what they're intending to do. Less people, more production.

Michael Moore

The purpose of the film is to show how General Motors, the world's largest corporation, destroyed its home town in a matter of eighteen months. (Laughs.) The working title is *Roger and Me*, meaning Roger Smith, a humorous look at how General Motors destroyed Flint, Michigan.

You think it's going to be very humorous?

Oh, yes. It's been a year full of laughs since I started filming this. We've got Pat Boone, Anita Bryant, you know, walking down the river with us telling us how to save Flint. We filmed the triumphant return of Bob Eubanks to Flint to do "The Newlywed Game"; he was born here. And so we got lots of funny stuff like that.

You know I'm being facetious, don't you?

And I'm writing a book, too. And this is all part of it.

There's somewhat of a sick sense of humor about it because it's pretty damn depressing and I don't want to ask people to sit in the dark for an hour and a half watching, you know (moans) this town crumble and people beat their wives and kill their neighbors and all the other things that make up our fine city.

So it's got to have either some humor or some hope.

Or a lesson.

Well, definitely it's a lesson for a lot of other places. It's too late for Flint, but maybe not too late for others. . . . The American Dream was you work hard, the company prospers, you prosper, right? Now it's, you work hard, the company prospers, you lose your job.

So you go out spend a day at Beecher High School, or Central or whatever and talk to kids there. Ask them what they got to look forward to here. Knowing they can't get out, they're trapped. All they got is McDonald's and selling drugs or go into the Army. Those are their three choices.

GM used to take pictures of their skilled trades apprentices, take 'em out to the schools as a career day item. They don't do that anymore either.

When we were in high school, Dad would bring home the applications. Ha, ha, ha. Right?

Inside Ethel's Bar

Walking into Ethel's Bar that afternoon was like walking into someone's memory, maybe a past life. People were just filtering in like the yellow light that leaned its arm along the dark bar rail. The owner was going out to make what might be his last bank deposit, while two waitresses dropped friendly hands on customers' shoulders. Someone had the idea the night before to sign the tops of the fake marble bar tables with a thick felt marker. Indelible curlicues proclaiming Eva and Joe '87, and Nick and Pauline Forever were never meant to leave their places. The talk was quiet except for the carping of "Brownie," a regular sitting alone at the front of the bar. Others pointed to him as one we should definitely interview.

Garry Brown

Let me sit up here [at the bar] next to you.

I don't care, you can sit on my face, I don't care. (Laughs.)

How long have you worked over there?

Fifteen and a half years.
    I got off work about noon thirty. About 12:30.

What are your plans? What are you going to do?

I'm not too sure what my plans are but what I want to know is how come Owen Bieber and Roger Smith don't have AIDS as much as they sleep together! I mean, you know, Jesus Christ, yeah, that's the way I feel. This last contract we got, tbe national contract, they didn't do a damn thing for the . . . there's thirty-seven hundred people that were forgotten, you know.

Hey. Bieber is still going to get his money. No matter what. Because he's president of the UAW. And in the paper the other day Roger Smith says we made more money last year and didn't make as many cars. You know. Billy Durant's* gotta' be doing flip-flops in his grave.

Oh yeah, they're making money. They bought EDS. Do you know why GM got EDS and California got the queers? California got first choice. You know.

If they hadn't bought out Perot, I'd love to see Perot stay in there. Because Perot was telling 'em right where the bear shit in the buckwheat. And Smith didn't like that. You know. That's the reason they got rid of Perot.

When they got rid of Perot they got rid of our profit-sharing, too. You know. Oh hell yes. Seven hundred-and-some-billion dollars down the tube to Perot. There went our profit-sharing just like [on] little wings. You know. Here I sit just like a duck flat-footed and don't give a fuck. Go ahead and take my picture (to a photographer).

Yeah. I got a wife and two kids. My oldest is eleven and my youngest is five years old.

How much warning did you get about the plant closing?

Um, actually four years ago. Oh yeah, they told us the plant was going to close, you know. And some people was going to Buick on 96 moves, see, seeing as how we was ceasing to make this certain job and they was going to Buick, we could follow 'em.

But you got all these bastards with twenty-five, twenty-eight, thirty years that don't want to retire. They went to Buick. So that left people like me out in the cold.

You know. And it just . . . but there was a bunch of people that moved to Buick. But . . . (to a friend) Goddamn look what the cat drug in the dog wouldn't touch! But there was . . . anyone with over twenty-eight years that went to Buick I feel was stupid be-

---

*Durant organized General Motors in 1905 and lost control of the company in 1920. He died in 1947.

cause they just give them the mutual retirement over here and they could have went out.

Can you get the Golden Handshake offer?

Oh yeah, I can get the Golden Handshake, yeah. But hey, I've got fifteen years invested with GM and all that. They only offered me $55,000 before taxes.

Then Uncle Sam gets his share of it and I end up with about $30,000. What the hell good is that going to do me? For my *life.*

Do any of your friends have plans for what they're going to do?

Oh, yeah, there's a lot of them, there's a lot of people that I work with that they're taking the Golden Handshake. Anybody below ten years [seniority], you know, I can see them taking the Golden Handshake.

But anybody above, you know, fifteen years like I got. But there's a lot of them that's taking it. And I can see them taking it. Because it's a good deal for them.

Do you have any advice for anybody in your situation? Or anything you'd like to say?

Yeah, sell all their GM stock and tell Roger Smith to stuff it in their ass.

Well, thank you, I don't want to disturb your day.

Well you ain't disturbed my day. Them bastards over there already did. What the hell.

Unknown Waitress

You've worked here how long?

Off and on eighteen years.

Is the primary reason you're closing because of the plant?

That's exactly the reason. All our trade is from these guys, it's all shop trade.

Did you ever think it would really close?

No. Never. For the last ten years, they've had rumors. You know. And for ten years, they're talking, but nobody ever believed it would happen. I still don't.

Have you had a lot of people come in the last week?

Yeah. People that did work here [Fisher] and went to Buick City. They've been coming back to say good-bye, you know. There'll be here yet. Buick City just now got off work. They'll be over. Yeah. Buick City will be here.

What are your plans?

I'm taking the winter off. See, I don't have to work. My husband works in the shop. I don't . . . you know. But this is where my friends are. If I had to depend on this for a living, I'm sure I'd be even more upset. But . . . He [my husband] worked over here [Fisher] for twenty years and then he got transferred over to Buick. He's got twenty-three.

So he's okay, though?

Well, we don't know. He's got twenty-three but they're getting closer . . .

Unknown Person with Nineteen Years

How long have you worked over there?

Nineteen years. Today's my last day.

What was the feeling over there?

Sad. It'll be sad tonight, too.

Did you ever think you'd see the whole plant close?

No. I didn't believe it. I did not believe it would ever happen.

Do you know what you're going to be doing?

I'm going to Buick City. I will eventually go to Buick City. Within the next year. I'm going on Paragraph 96. It's the negotiated contract. Yes. I got eight more years to go and then I'm going to retire.

I've got a lot of friends that ain't going to have jobs. It's sad for them. She [points to Jane Williams] took a buy-out. And a lot of the younger ones are taking the buy-out.

You got history that was built here. Durant built it. It was history. And this is part of history, no matter what happens.

Well, GM knows what they're doing, I believe. But you know, somebody thinks they . . . But I don't know.

What are the others doing, who don't have jobs or buy-outs?

OTHER WOMAN: They're going to be on welfare.

Yeah. Some of them are going to school. Majority will end up on welfare, yeah. The ones with seven, eight years.

UNKNOWN PERSON: I'm going to. I'll end up on welfare and I got fifteen years.

Unknown Person

My thoughts have been the fact of what a great town Flint was when it was booming. We all thought GM was it. You got in there. You made a great living. Everybody had everything. And now it's going to be a welfare city.

Do you know what you're going to do?

I'm hoping to work with computers somehow. I have this far-fetched dream of doing it in my own home so I don't have to punch a clock no more. But I want to be a writer, too. I've felt so much about this story that I though this would be a good opportunity to write a story about what I thought about the plant closing. And if it was published, it would be a start.

Twelve years. I didn't have to take the buy-out. I just don't see a future with GM. Yesterday was my last day. Second shift. That's why we're so tired today.

First shift was supposed to have a big party over at Embers but nobody's there yet. Maybe they changed it to Little Caesar's. Sometime today I'm sure there's going to be a lot of people.

Lot of terrific, terrific customers. Even now. Monday night a whole bunch of them fellow bar owners come in to wish me off. Everybody has their own crews.

See, I catered strictly to the shop. I didn't cater to no bums off the streets, stuff like that. Where some of the bars down the strip do. So now, they'll survive but I got to go down with the tubes, that's all.

That guy next door, now, he'll survive. He caters to a younger crowd and stuff like that.

It's just a regular shop bar. It's a good bar. It was. And we're going to miss all the people, I tell you. It's . . . we've got the best customers in the world.

Even the detective was in today, he says, You know, I never, ever, hear a call for your place. I said, That's cause we got good customers, you know. We never have trouble in here. We just never do.

He's a nephew of one of my good customers who's in the hospital with cancer, so he stopped by just to let me know about it. Real good customer.

Do you have any advice for anybody about the bar business?

Don't get in it now. It's a bad business right now. Insurances, and stuff. Come license renewal time it'll be mandatory insurance and that's going to close down a lot of bars that can't afford insurance.

We won't be able to renew our license unless we post a $50,000 bond or insurance to get our license and that's going to knock the little guy right out of the picture. There's a lot of guys don't have insurance now. That's probably, I'd say, eighty percent of the bar owners don't have insurance.

My only advice is treat the customers good and they treat you good. It's just like one guy brought me in a painting last night of his cat. He did it himself, and I mean it is a beautiful painting. I mean, I didn't even know the guy had any talents, you know? Just to give us 'cause he liked us. He said, Something to remember me by.

Last night, that was the biggest send off we ever had. If the fire marshal would have come by last night he would have closed us up for sure. (Laughs.) Thank God he didn't, I tell you. I just couldn't believe it.

3

The Korner Bar

*The Korner Bar is ten feet from Ethel's Bar. The people at the bar
are used to the media by now and spot us as we come in to ask
our questions. It's obvious we're not regulars. But they're very
polite. This bar is wider than Ethel's and more "upscale"—or
maybe it's just better lighting. The clientele is somewhat younger but the mood here is the same: controlled anxiety, a sad
cameraderie.*

*One guy with a flat hat and a long look hunches over the
end of the bar holding a half-smoked cigarette, nursing a shot-
glass. He looks like he's seen everything and taken it all at face
value. A straight shooter. We are told he is the owner.*

Roy Hughey

How long have you owned this bar?

Ten years.

Did you ever think the plant would really close?

Well, not until recently, no. I mean, we've finally had to accept
the fact. Probably in the last year or so, but prior to that we kept
thinking, Yeah, there'll be something come in, it won't close.

That was the whole thing; we figured they'd bring something
in, maybe not comparable to what they did have—but something.

Are you a shop bar? Is that who you cater to?

Yeah.

Why are you staying open?

Well, what choice do I have? I've retired from the shop seven years ago, but I've got my investment in here and there's no way to get it out. So, I might as well stay here and see if I can make it go.

That's what we're hoping—that we can draw in some other clientele, off-the-street clientele as well as some of the locals, and maybe survive.

We've had several people from Buick come back over for the last couple of days. Just more or less I guess out of sympathy, getting close to Christmas and people want to say Hi and Hello to their old friends and Have a nice holiday and this type of thing.

But it's . . . I really don't know how to explain it but it's . . . I know it's sincere feelings. Friendship from people that they've worked with over a period of years.

I grew up in Flint and I can't believe it's closing, either.

Yeah. I think that's true with everybody. It's due to the fact it's been here so long, it's been more or less a trademark of Flint, Fisher Body. Seems like it goes back forever and everybody seems to think that it should still be here. But unfortunately, it's not going to be. It's all done now.

Do you see bringing in other clients?

I'm hoping to bring in enough to be able . . . I've got two boys that work here and I hope they can make a living out of it because there's no jobs available in Flint. They both worked for me since they got out of school. And they don't have anything else to go to.

If they can make a living out of it, fine. Then I'll be satisfied. Not happy, but satisfied.

Where did your work for GM?

Right here, Fisher 1. I retired after thirty years.

You must have a lot of friends who are leaving GM today. What's the feeling do you think?

I think it's more disillusionment, just a letdown you know. They're not really bitter. But there's a certain amount of anger. They have some harsh feelings, but I don't think at anybody. But the economy as a whole, at General Motors.

Because I think the general consensus is that General Motors is putting the works to Flint. They've taken everything out of Flint and . . .

My personal thinking on that is that due to the high concentration of organized labor, I think they're trying to get away from that. And this plant here is very historical in the UAW union movement and I think that's part of their goal is to get away from the high concentration of unionized labor and get back to more or less nonunion workers and have more control themselves over what their total operation is.

You look like you've got a great bar.

We've enjoyed it, and this bar itself has a lot of history. It's been here for a long time. It started right after Prohibition.

I can't tell you the exact year, but I know different people . . . In fact there was a guy in here today that worked here when they got the first beer license and he said it was right after Prohibition.

A friend of mine who died a couple of years ago used to come in here regular, all the time. He worked here when the guy that owned it as a restaurant got the beer license. And he said he bought the first beer that was ever bought in here. But he couldn't remember the year for sure. Mid-thirties, some time after Prohibition.

So, this bar goes way back and there's a lot of old people that come here. Just very dedicatedly. For years. Now a lot of them, a lot of the old retirees, now some of them are still living, but they're up in years and their health's bad or whatever. So we don't get much of them in here.

When I first took over the place we had quite a crowd still coming and they used to come in to play euchre. I had a card license and we had euchre tournaments and things going on the weekends. During the winter it was really, really something. Gave them a place to go. Some place to socialize with their friends, you know.

But it just . . . that group of people . . . some of 'em died, and some of 'em are up in years and their health's failing them and one thing and another, so we lost most of that crowd. They do come in once in a while.

I've been coming here myself since back in the mid-fifties.

How did you get to own the bar?

Well, I was getting to within five years of retiring. Or at least possible retirement. Thirty years is an option. You can take it or not. And I had to think about that seriously, Do I want to get out? Am I able to get out? Am I financially stable?

And so I thought, by making some kind of an investment, getting something going besides just retirement, that would be the way to do it. And the only way that I could see.

So that's what I invested in here and I was here three and a half years before I retired. I bought into it before I retired and I knew the two previous owners real well. One of them was a friend of mine for twenty-some odd years, even before he came in here, the last owner. And the other guy I knew for probably eleven years. So I knew pretty much what the bar was like and what to expect.

So it was a new experience really for me because I'd never been in business before. I had a tremendous amount of things I didn't know. But knowing the person I bought it from, the last owner, even though he didn't stay in Flint—he went to Tawas—but he was available. I could contact him if I run into problems.

So it made it a little easier. It wasn't like just going into something blind.

Do you have any advice for anybody who's getting out?

No, I don't. In Flint, right now, it doesn't look that good. I mean the total economic situation is bad. And I don't see any chance of it getting better in the immediate future. Naturally, we all hope it gets better down the road, but in the next couple to three or four years, I don't see any chance of things getting any better.

So for young people that don't have any time I'd say they should be looking at other places. Unless there's something as far as going into business for themselves here, something that they know is going to last.

There's some talk [about relocating] but I think everybody right now is—hasn't really felt the complete, the full impact yet.

They're waiting to see what's really going to happen, what it's going to be like. And probably there will be a lot of decisions made from this point on.

It's not like having a job, but they'll have some security, some little bit of benefits going on, employment and SUB-pay, so whatever time that lasts. And then this GIS program, which I don't know how well that's going to work out.

I can't believe in my own mind that General Motors is going to go into the welfare business and give these people so much money for the rest of their life, but by the same token, they may be able to come up with some jobs for them in other areas if not here.

Do you have any advice, anything that you'd like to say to people?

No, I think I've said it all.

PART 2

LIFE AFTER THE LINE

Carriero

Tom Carriero, who gave his age as fortyish, has worked more than twenty years at General Motors, mostly at Chevrolet Manufacturing, before starting his own business, Hartland Balloons From the Air, Inc.

His well-managed business, which employs at least three others on a full-time basis, provides an advertising and entertainment service through his patented remote control hot-air balloons. The service can be used during half-time at hockey and football games or for advertising. He planned to take his balloons to the 1988 Olympics in Calgary as part of the opening ceremonies. Not bad for a company still in its first year.

He was interviewed in his comfortable office, part of a six room building with lobby and small demonstration area.

He is unmarried and looks younger than his more than forty years, a self-possessed man who talks slowly and deliberately.

Unlike many others, he voluntarily quit General Motors to pursue his own business. The difference between discussing his former job at General Motors and his new business is like the difference between grease and gold.

I started work at General Motors on September 21, 1967, at the Chevrolet Flint Manufacturing and I worked on the line loading parts. And as I got my ninety days in, I started looking around for other things to do in the factory besides standing there putting parts in the baskets all day.

I looked for a better job and moved up into truck driving and then crane operating and that kind of stuff.

Some people do the same thing for maybe two years and then move because they get bored with their work.

I wanted to be moved.

I haven't been laid off as far as this business goes. I've quit the factory, okay, so there's a little bit of difference.

Along with being moved around, I became popular and got very involved in the union. I started in the union as a alternate committeeman and I've held various union positions for the past fifteen years from the alternate to the UAW co-director for the Human Resource Department at our location.

In the interim, I received a lot of education through General Motors and the UAW. Business education. Union background. All those.

Being a co-director for the Human Resource Center I went through management courses to see what the other side of the fence was like, aside from union. And the inner conflict between the union and management, the politics that were involved prompted me to start my own business.

(Lower, softly.) There was a lot of back-stabbing between the union and management. Within the union, within management. A lot of politics. I got tired of trying to do the right things and somebody coming behind you, or somebody being over you changed the course of action that you set, according to people that elected you to do your job.

The key, I guess, the key to some of the politicians' success is flexibility. You know. They change the rules a lot. Well.

What prompted me was . . . (Tightly) . . . I want to say this but I'll implicate a lot of things . . . An incident came up in an election year for our local union officers. I was not satisfied with the results of the election myself, personally.

I accept responsibility and do my job well when I have a job to do.

The incident that triggered me to make a move was the outcome of the election. I could see where the future of the union and General Motors Corporation was taking our particular plant. At our location we went from close to twelve thousand people down to three thousand.

I understand the need to do things efficiently and to cut costs. What I did not understand is the way it was being done. It was being done at the employee's expense.

And the transition period that the people had to go through from not replacing people through attrition to layoffs, and the burden that was left with the people there to manufacture the parts properly and the equipment and the management . . .

See, management at our location got real confident in their business in the sixties and seventies. But it has still been management's responsibility to run the plant and the union to help them.

Everybody got lax, which put out a poor quality product. The Japanese took advantage of that. Chrysler Corporation. Ford Motors. And as a result, you can see where General Motors has lost and they are not number one any more.

Well. My attitude toward employment, for creating a new job or doing whatever, is that if there's a problem, there's a solution and you do it, whatever it may be.

So. I just walked out of there one day, said, I'm never coming back in here. I'm going to make this business work. I developed a product. I took a personal leave. Now I'm on a formal leave. I've submitted for the Golden Handshake to collect on my retirement.

I have no intentions of going back in the shop. Even if this business fails. I have no intention of going back in there.

You know, there's a lot of detail that goes into elections and the union politics and the dedication and everything but the one thing that broke my back was the outcome of the election.

I felt that some of the candidates that were elected along with some of the employment officers and the reorganization structure that we were in were a move to break the union's back. The corporation and the attempts that were being made by some dedicated individuals on both sides did not dictate the future success of the corporation.

That's my opinion. And that has held true . . . Look around us to the auto industry.

I don't want to work with somebody who's not competent to perform their job. And there are a lot of people that are involved on the union and management side in the plants that are incompetent.

And I refused to put myself in a position of working with people that don't have the competency level to perform their task or duties. There was too much of that through favoritism and politics on both sides of the fence.

I understand that's business. But it doesn't make business sense to watch your own organization be destroyed because of favoritism and politics. And our organization—speaking General Motors, UAW—is being destroyed by incompetent people.

I'm talking about what happened in the auto industry and how they lost, okay?

My feelings are that it started with General Motors when the oil embargo started, the downsizing of cars. The gas crunch. Right in that area. The other thing was the presidential election. When Ronald Reagan took office and fired the airline traffic controllers, it opened the door to all corporations on union activities and they put the hammer down.

A few people in management said: Aha! We can do something here that will slow the union down. And coupled with the economy, oil embargo, a lot of things contributed to what I call the downfall of the auto industry.

No matter how well I do my job, it's not going to matter because that's not what they're interested in.

(Slowly, softly.) That's correct. Right. As hard as individuals worked, we had no say because we didn't get to call the shots that would probably make GM a lot more successful. They just said, That is what we have to do.

The one thing that we all lost sight of was the quality of work that's put out through the door. That's what beat the auto industry. It was quality of work that was put out the door.

Our foreign competition. In the beginning everybody laughed at them. They emphasized quality as they grew after we taught them our technology. We taught them. They took advantage of that and when the foreign industry started putting out quality products . . .

They started listening to some of the speakers that came from America. Dr. Demming is one of them. He's a quality expert.

And General Motors told Dr. Demming, We don't need you. Dr. Demming went overseas, started something in the auto industry in Japan. Japan immediately saw what Dr. Demming and other quality expects were talking about, and immediately changed their manufacturing process and started producing quality products.

The oil embargo came in. Fuel started to be rationed. Which threw the auto industry here into—What do we do? Let's make subcompact cars. And the subcompact cars from General Motors industry were poor quality.

From there on out it went downhill. (Long pause.)

Do you feel that if people working on the line had more to say about production, if they had been given more input, do you think it would have been a different story? More quality?

Yes. I do.

We have struggled for that say in the corporation. That is something that is finally being recognized through our joint process. You know, that the UAW leadership is getting to have more say. But the negotiations that took place between the corporation and the UAW gave us the flexibility to make business decisions in the plant. And those are the things that we are fighting for.

I believe in the union. I believe in what the union stands for. There are a lot of things that need to be changed. There always is change. Without change in any organization, it dies. It becomes boring.

"We've always done it this way."

Right. Management's position was they weren't willing to change. And our position was now, we're going to make a change one way or another. It's necessary to do that.

When the change came, the layoffs, do you think there was anything that GM could have done to make that transition easier? Training programs, education, etc.?

People have not taken advantage of the training programs offered by the union and management although some have. A few. The plan's there. The money's there.

I guess you have to understand why blue-collar workers are blue-collar workers. They don't want the responsibility . . . of running their own business. They want to feel comfortable working for someone else.

That goes along with the blue-collar worker. That goes along with their lack of interest in training programs offered by General Motors. The transition from being laid-off—from working to being laid-off—for some of those people that are on unemployment and for those people that have no more unemployment, depended on other people doing things for them.

Now, that's their responsibility. Those people that you hear say General Motors and the union don't have programs, they don't do this and don't do that. It's their lack of interest and self-motivation to better themselves in life.

They want to just get by.

That's people's motivation—lack of it.

I was setting at the plant one day and I thought, there are so many people in America that have done silly things and become millionaires. Over a pet rock, the hula hoop, right?

Well, I set there with those thoughts in mind. I knew I had a product, back in the beginning, that if it was developed would be a valuable marketing tool for advertisers.

And knowing that America is the land of opportunity and knowing that a lot of other people went out and did what they did and became successful . . .

The only reason they became successful was the fact that

nobody else did it. They did it. Like nobody else is doing what I'm doing.

I am the first in the country to open this type of business. You have to do those things yourself and build yourself a team of people that will work with you.

Like my involvement with the union over the years. The team effort was the thing that made the union successful. And that's what I'm doing with my business. I built a team effort here.

I've had a lot of hobbies in the last twenty years and one of them is radio-controlled airplanes.

I started a year ago in March. I went to the largest radio controllers show in the United States. They had everything from little cars to big cars and airplanes and I found a radio-controlled balloon. It was like a hot-air balloon. And I became interested in it.

I bought a set of plans from a designer and I put a unit together and went out and started flying. Well, the balloons were nice and I enjoyed the sport but they had poor directional control.

The onboard flight system had to be developed further than what it was.

I began developing that along with some of the people that I had been involved with in the hobby industry. Through many hours of developing this system, we came up with a commercial product that can be used indoors or outdoors.

I've got a patent pending number at this time and I've formed a corporation. Yes, this is in operation.

Through the course of the business and the search for graphics on our balloons, I met with Cameron Balloons in Ann Arbor, Michigan, the people that run that business.

The Cameron Balloons people knew someone who made replica balloons, freestanding, that were filled by inflator fans. Those balloons did not fly. That person had a business in Minnesota.

The graphics that the lady could put on the balloons were far superior to anything or anyone in the United States has done as far as replicas.

Through negotiations I bought that company and moved it here to Michigan.

The name of her business was Heartland Balloons and the name of my business was From the Air, Inc. Indoor Advertising. Well, the whole project was a natural. Her balloons and my flight systems.

So we called the business Hartland Balloons From the Air Incorporated.

This was not a slow investment. I actually started this business at the end of last March, working on the project from March to December 31st. We put close to $100,000 in this business.

I'll give you a little history of the way the company's going at this time.

We officially started in March, April. Somewhere in there we developed the product line. Then, through bringing Heartland Balloons here, the lady, she knows the grandfathers of ballooning: Don Picard, the world record holders, Chapman. She has the ballooning history and community behind her model replica balloons. The list of her contacts through her business building the replicas is unlimited.

She has America's best painter. The man is an artist. He paints murals on balloons. I believe he has fifty balloons in the world that he has painted. One of those balloons is called the Good News Balloon.

The Good News Balloon is a seven-story hot-air balloon with thirty feet high, three-story murals painted on it. Of Calvary with the three crosses, Mother Mary and the Baby Jesus, the Praying Hands and those kinds of things on the Good News Balloon.

He and the woman worked together for four years. They became personal friends. She is very dedicated to reproducing those seven-story balloons.

The contacts that she has really support what we're doing through the ballooning community 'cause now all of a sudden we can fly those balloons.

We have made arrangements through some of the balloon manufacturers and the painter and the owner of the Good News balloon. It is going to be the Hare Balloon in the Hare and Hound Race at the opening ceremonies for the 1988 Olympics in Calgary, Canada.

We are manufacturing a replica, an eight-foot model. We will be flying our replica model of the Good News Balloon in the opening ceremonies in Calgary. I am going to be in the seven-story Good News Balloon, piloting our radio-controlled balloon around the Good News Balloon. It is the first balloon for the opening ceremony launch. To go up 150 feet and that is the center of the contest.

The Olympics.

The motivation for me was: I cannot . . . I'm looking for the right word . . . I have too much energy to have someone give me a job that is a routine job, I guess.

I have organizational abilities. I've got all the background to run the business and make all the right contacts, and so that's pretty much now why I'm here.

I've worked twenty hours a day on some days. We're projected to do three million dollars of business by December 31, 1988. And that's pretty good for the first year.

The best advice that I could give anybody would be: Take charge of your own life. Make your own decisions. Develop the skills necessary to perform whatever function you want and continue educating yourselves in your field.

A person's motivation, I guess, comes from within.

But you control your own destiny. And a lot of people point the finger at someone else. *Why isn't this done or why isn't that done?* If you won't get down there and do something yourself in business, don't ask somebody else to do it.

I like being creative and motivated. I'm highly motivated. I like just getting involved in things. The automobile situation coupled with the political situation and the management situation . . . I wanted to do something creative. I'm a take charge type of person. That's all there is to it.

I'll give you a breakdown here of what goes on. There are followers. There are leaders. There are leaders of leaders. And leaders of leaders of leaders. We all fall into a category. I feel that I'm a leader.

I'm not the guy at the back of the crowd, you know, I'm the guy in front. I'm thirsty for knowledge. Whatever that is, whatever subject. I like to listen and learn.

This is a very difficult business to start, keeping in mind nobody in the whole world is doing what we're doing. This is not something like opening a grocery store or a Seven-Eleven, you know. This is a very, very different business. It's unusual.

I have found it difficult to get into areas to fly indoors like in sports arenas and malls.

First of all I say, I want to fly my balloon in here. *Huh? What are you talking about? No!*

Then after you do the demonstration, they open the door.

But I beat on the Pontiac Silverdome for six months before I got in. It is an ideal place for it, but they didn't know what to do with us because it's a new means of advertising, a new way to make money.

One thing I found where we've had a hard time is when the people who are influential don't let us in. The ones that have advertising rights in most buildings. They're really upset 'cause they didn't come up with the idea to do this.

We've got the patent pending number and the whole bit. We're on our way. There's nobody in the country, the world, prepared to do what we're doing.

Some were easier to convince. Some of the hockey teams

jumped right into it for entertaining people. You know, you've got your hockey games, basketball games, professional football and baseball and you have breaks in there with nothing to do. What do you do?

Well, now they got something to look at. A show. And it entertains the fans. And that's what it's about. It's entertaining. Our product is entertaining. And it gets your message there.

I'm really excited about what we're doing, I believe in it.

I'm going to avoid rock concerts. I'll do concerts but not rock and roll. People throw stuff at our balloons and it's a rougher crowd. We did a rock concert, not a rock concert, but rock for one of the local area radio stations' birthdays. We flew at the Hyatt Regency for the first time and we had Mitch Ryder there and people got kind of loose. And people were throwing stuff at the balloons, trying to jump up and get it.

I'm not going to take a chance jeopardizing equipment and the people involved, although a five-foot balloon totally loaded weighs only two pounds. There's nothing that's going to hurt anyone. But if it was knocked out of the air, I'm not going to take the chance of destroying my equipment.

We've done a lot of research and we are now going to be able to deal internationally through the Olympics. We're going to be a worldwide business.

Ballooning communities looked for this for years—for replica, radio-controlled balloons. They have opening ceremonies usually for the Olympics, starts with 150 hot-air balloons on a launch and everything just went naturally with what we're doing. So it's why we were asked.

I like my business. The motivation that makes me work harder is to not go back into the shop.

Two things make people change. One of them is conflict. When you have conflict, there's going to be a change one way or the other. Between two people, two organizations, husband and wife, cats and dogs. There's a conflict and it causes change.

The other thing is the willingness and desire of the person to change. If those three elements, the willingness, the desire, and the motivation are there, people will change.

They will evolve from where they're at and move forward. And that's the only advice. Be open-minded and have the willingness to change.

It's hard 'cause people get in a rut.

I love what I'm doing.

I went through a successful career as a union official who never lost an election. That's because I did my job.

To run my own business, has it changed me? Ah, I'm me. It's just me. My thirst to become involved with things that . . . I've always wanted to learn from people. And talk to them. Those older people have a lot of knowledge to share with us. If you take the time to sit down and talk to them, they'll teach you.

I hired in the shop in 1967. I learned from the grandfathers of the union. I listened to them. I went to school and educated myself. I wanted to know more and more and more. Now I just channel that into the ballooning community, you know.

You're as good as your teachers. If you surround yourself with all the best, you'll come out that way.

It's pretty much how I evolved in this business.

It was a transition for me to go from a General Motors type or factory type of situation. My whole family, grandfather, grandmother, aunts and uncles, mom, everybody encouraged working in the factories. Because it was a secure future and a good income. A sure bet and why take a chance?

And I listened to my family to their advice. And it was good advice at the time. Nobody paid as good money. Nobody offered insurance. I was a young kid. What did I know? Okay, I'll go in the shop.

And the transition from—how do you say it—from being automotive oriented and programmed by your family that this is what you've got to do because it's good for you, to making my own decision that it's good for some, but not good for me, because that's not me. It was hard for me to explain.

And it was great for me after I made the decision. But that transition period was tough.

I had thought about it for the last two years that I worked there. But I just didn't know what I was going to do. And finally, you know, I sat there and said after all the time, the outcome of the election, I thought, it's time to do it whatever it is. I'm going to go for it.

And I went for it. I listened to people. Older people. I listened to everyone. Young and old. Listening and learning is where it's at.

My lifestyle may change as the business prospers. But I won't change. I'll always be me. It doesn't matter how much money I get or whatever happens. I'll still always want to learn and want to work and that kind of stuff. And be a leader.

One of the nice things about this new business is I'm working with the rehabilitation and labor market consultant for handicapped people. We're going to be able to have some handicapped pilots that fly the remotes and we need baskets weaved and that kind of stuff. And I've made some arrangements with a gentleman from this organization to start employing the handicapped.

I just feel like I've got so much to add to the community and nationally to all communities.

It's like having a baby. This business is like having a baby. It's got its own personality and you have to nurture it just like you do a kid.

I was satisfied with what I was doing in the union because it was progressive. I made $65,000 a year in the shop plus an expense account. I did okay in the shop. But I guess I was moving too fast.

Right now, the element of surprise is with this company, with what we're doing. Then we hit the Olympics *schooo* that's it, we're world-wide.

When I fly that balloon in the Olympics we'll get world recognition with this product.

And we have a choice. We're either going to create our own competition, or they will join us in being successful and want to franchise our product and buy franchises from us.

We're going to grow rapidly and we're looking—we're scheduling January 18 through the 21st—a New Orleans presentation to twenty-eight states to offer them franchises . . . Our projections, that's that three million plus.

If everything goes according to plan, in projections, we should be well over five million in total sales in franchises and flight time by the end of the year.

Being first in what we're doing is like the Kleenex tissues. There's been a lot of people come and go trying to duplicate Kleenex, but they're still here.

We're seven, eight months ahead of everybody right now.

Everything's kind of up in the air, you know. (Laughs)

It's exciting because nobody's ever done it. I do want to be first with what I'm doing with this project. That's what makes it exciting. If you slow down now, you're going to get run over. There's no time for that.

We've been approached by investors. We've been offered two million dollars for the business. I've needed some funds but I deal through a bank. I don't want to get what is called venture capitalists. I don't want somebody setting down telling me, Hey, you're doing this wrong and that wrong.

I'm not going to stand and argue with a board of directors or anybody about the course of action that I want the company to go.

By mid-march, we'll have probably $500,000. So we don't need the investments now.

When we get to the Olympics. That's going to be unreal.

After all, when a balloon goes by, the whole world stops to watch.

POSTSCRIPT: *Although he did not fly his balloon at the opening ceremonies of the 1988 Olympics in Calgary because of bad weather conditions, he did manage to sell several franchises and deemed the trip worthwhile. He has since sold his company and is vice-president of a similar company.*

Sullivan

Michele Sullivan, thirty-eight, wore blue jeans and a silk jacket emblazoned with Local 599 as she officiated at that local's meeting, where more than two hundred laid-off workers sat, listening intently. Topics included a new University of Michigan–Flint training program, unemployment, and SUB-pay benefits. A credit counselor was on hand to explain how to manage debts and stave off home foreclosures for the workers on "indefinite" layoff.

It was a far cry from proud union endorsements or strike and arbitration meetings. But an air of helpfulness prevailed in the hall. Most of the union officials organizing the programs were themselves laid off, like Michele.

Although laid off since August 7, 1987, a date she never forgets, Michele continues to serve her local as chairwoman of the Women's Committee. She is paid daily expenses and travel, though she does not receive wages. She works to bring programs and options to others in her situation.

She has two children—Tammy, seventeen, and Tina, nineteen—and a nine-month-old grandson named Bryce. She is divorced and the sole support of the family.

Michele wears her dark reddish hair in shiny lobe-length curls that frame her lightly freckled face and teal, contact-capped eyes. She speaks in a full, gravelly voice and frequently pauses, as if fixing each point firmly before her listener. She described the highlights of several different jobs she has held in her eleven and a half years with General Motors, beginning with her final release from Plant 81, Buick City, where something called "The New Concept" was part of her orientation and theory of plant work life.

Her job, until recently, had been quality control.

About two weeks before we got laid off they called a special meeting in the back of the plant. They had set up the chairs, microphones. You know—Come in. Told us all to be there. We all set there. And they said, "Well we have to reduce schedule." And yet, we just got a new bid on a new job.

And they told us, "Well, August 7 we're going to level out."

And we set there and the committeeman told us to all be quiet. Don't ask no questions. Just let them say their little spiel and get up and go back to work.

Well, in this little conversation, head honcho, says um, "You've done a f-i-i-ne job for the last five years. Now get out and don't come back." Basically.

We had two weeks to decide right? Two weeks. So the last day of work, the week before we were to get laid off, I told my advisor, "If you don't need me after August 7th, you don't need me between now and August 7th. I want a vacation." My first vacation in eleven and a half years. Never, never taken a vacation.

So he told me he would fire me if I took a vacation.

I had to call the committeeman even though I said, "Look, I've never had a vacation, I'd like to take a vacation."

So. That was just—I knew two weeks before that I was going to get laid off indefinitely. Only two weeks. And I just went nuts. I went nuts. If the committeeman hadn't told me not to say anything I would have got up and chewed him out royally. Because I bought into that plant. I didn't get shipped down. I didn't get reduced in. I give up a super good job for more pay.

My first two months I did nothing but cry. I cried for two months straight. And my daughter, Tammy, just couldn't understand why I was crying. Why I was depressed. "Mom, you got time to spend with me." "Great. Where's the money to spend any time with you now?" You know.

See, when I first started in the shop I had nothing. I lived in a little two-bedroom apartment, with a few amounts of furniture, barely a black and white TV. Nothing. But within a matter of a year, I'd gotten a car, I'd gotten furniture, I'd gotten just as much as my brother did and he'd been in there twenty-some years.

Then, what do you spend the money on? Finally, they come out with a fat lady shop. I spent my money on clothes. I swore that I would never be in polyester pants again.

I've yet to be in a pair of polyester pants.

I would never wear purple again. Because I always wore purple polyester pants. I have gotten VCRs and microwaves and freezers and deep-freezers and brand-new stove, brand-new refrigerator.

I could go out and get it with a sign of my name. I loved it. And now I have the fear that I'm going to lose everything I've got.

See, we've already had a suicide at Buick. That never even entered my mind. I had no idea that anybody would ever commit suicide because they lost a job. Why? You know? There would never be anything that drastic to make me take my own life. Not over a job. But yet, there are people out there that will.

I didn't know them [the suicide]. I was at a meeting for stress management that's going to be put on December 18 at the union hall. And yes, we've had one suicide at Buick already. Successful suicide. Right after they got laid off, when they heard they'd never get called back.

See, everybody else that I know has worked before the shop. I never worked before the shop. A week as a secretary for a company that was folding. Two or three days as a telephone solicitor, which I never got paid for. Worked as a waitress in a bar for two weeks and quit in the middle of a shift.

Eight years. Eight years could be a long time. They [the suicide] didn't have ten years. So they were thinking, Everything's gone.

My mom and I . . . right after I got laid off and I was still in my super-depressed state of crying. I said, "Ma, you know, I don't know what I'm good at. I'm thirty-eight years old and I don't know what I can do, what I'm even qualified for."

I don't know what's out there. I haven't been out in the job market for eleven and a half years.

I only got hired at the shop on a bet. That's the only reason I'm in the shop. The guy I was with, he said, "You ain't cool enough to go to work." On a bet, on a dare I went down there, went down the next day, filled out my application, took my physical.

They said, "Can you come to work tomorrow?" (Laughs.) I wasn't ready, you know. I was twenty-seven. I'd never had a job really, nothing to speak of, nothing to fall back on as far as employment or anything.

Well, now they tell me that I might get back in the shop. I might. Well, I'm not out here to hang on a "might." I don't want to hang on a "might."

I want to be a little more independent. I want to be something else.

When my brother got me in the shop, he told me I would only get fifteen years in, anyway. But I wasn't counting on eleven and a half years, I was counting on fifteen years in. Because when I hit my ten years I said okay, I'll finance my car for five more years,

I'll pay off my solar system in five years, pay off my new furnace, I'll pay off my house, I'll do this, I'll do this, I'll do this.

I had been planning since day one that I only had fifteen years to get in. But I was counting on them fifteen years. I was never going to be in there more than fifteen years. For the simple reason, my brother has never given me any false information yet.

I mean I had such a good job. I was extra set-up person. Everybody came in all the time. So you know what I got to do, don't you? Talk to everybody. [It was] right across the street—Plant 31.

Okay, so. The last day for the sign up of this plant—they called it buying in—I went down there. I got out of work at 6 A.M. in the morning, went down there, waited around until 8:00.

This is—boom-boom—one day into the next.

Well, I went into work and it was the job I had already taught everybody who had already went to 81. All the jobs in my department which, my department made the same product we were now making in 81. Okay, so I had to take groups and groups and groups of people through teaching them the individual jobs. Showing them how to set up the Saginaws. The only ones I didn't know was the Maspect. I didn't like messing around with nitrogen. Okay. That's the only one I didn't care to learn. The guy always was there, so I didn't have to know.

But I knew the welding machines, the brake-ons, the R and Bs, everything. I was training people to learn these jobs over in Plant 81.

I had lost high pay to go to low pay. In the new plant you had to learn two complete units of jobs to get your high pay.

I said, "How about if I just go around and show you that I know the jobs?" He said, "Well, you're going to have to call a meeting for that."

So I called a meeting. We went in the Oasis. I said, "Look, you know that I trained you over there. On my shift. You give me the specs and I'll set em up, run 'em, show you a perfect part." Sure.

I took them around to every machine that was on the floor. The only one I didn't know was the Excello and the Foxstop cause them were ancient, ancient machines which we didn't have over there [at the previous plant]. We had Saginaws, and other different types of machines that did the work. Like boring out for the insert pin and you know, this stuff.

So I took them around and I ran all perfect parts on all the machines except the Foxstop and the Excello. The Foxstop was in one group. The Excello was in another. Okay. So. They said we'll give you your first nickel raise today in both units.

So that made me a dime. A dime more an hour. So I got in there. Norman taught me the job. Nothing to it. It was the same as the other machines except it was laying flat instead of going up and down. That was all the difference. So there wasn't really nothing to learn on it.

The Foxstop was a machine where you put a part on and take a part off at the same time and in between you push buttons. Okay, so it's you slip it on, push your buttons, take off the part, guage it, put it on the line to go down 'cause it was good. And change all the tools which was nothing. It was easy for me. The names just scared me because I'd never heard of 'em before.

So I got that one down. He taught me both of them that night. And I called a meeting again. And I got my high pay the next day.

And Michele's all done with her schedule, been done with her schedule. Two and a half hours I can run six hundred parts no problem.

So I went over to pumps. I started working and at that time it was manual setting veins with your hands because the gilmans had not been set in.

[I wanted that] because that was my favorite job. That was my favorite job out of 31 [previous plant she worked at]. Setting veins. You take thirty-one veins in your hand and you got a wheel in front of you, a little turntable kind of thing, and choo-choo-choo-choo (imitates the sound of an air gun) I could set 'em. I could set 'em. They called me the human gilman. (Laughs.)

We were supposed to run eleven trays a day and in the trays you were supposed to get fifty an hour was what they said an average worker could do. But I was doing like a hundred—the same as a machine would do. (Proudly.)

And I could just set 'em real fast and I was done.

I'd already had high pay, but I had to show 'em that I knew, so I went through and showed 'em you know, I took my . . . they rotated the job. You worked this job for a week then you go to this job for a week and then this job for a week until you hit all the jobs and then you come back.

Well, some fine person in our unit decided that we should pick permanent jobs. I was already specialized but I picked indent load because I lost eighteen pounds in six weeks. Just from working on it. Just from working . . . it was one of the hardest jobs.

We were doubling up on it and the schedule was five thousand

and I loaded four thousand by myself every day or every other day I should say.

Where the other guy would load uh, one thousand parts which is a basket and a half and you can feed them up that line and into them sixteen machines like this (moves her hands quickly) you know.

But I was loading four thousand every other day which was great. I enjoyed it.

And so I went on the job and it took me about two and a half hours to load four thousand parts and I was done and gone. And then I just last year, Memorial Day or Labor Day, I was going with this guy and he's on second [shift]. Although he could have been on third or first, he was twenty years seniority.

Well, between one day and the next we broke up. No lovin', no huggin', no kissin', just—go on home.

And he just went on about his merry way and I was stuck with second. I'd already lost thirty dollars a week by going from third to second, okay? And uh, this one girl and I finally became partners on the same job.

We shared three machines. We worked it out she'd go first one day I'd go first one day, back and forth. She started out well, do three hundred of mine and tomorrow I'll pay you back three hundred. So I would run one thousand, she would run four hundred (laughs), you know.

And we kept trading back and forth and it got all right. Marsha and I never had a fight once we became partners on the job. But we fought every day on third shift. Every day on third shift. I mean it was—she's Polish—and her and I just didn't get along on third shift. She didn't think I—well, on third shift I was always drunk. Always drunk.

Why? If you had to be up all night long what were you going to do? Right? I'd been busted in after-hour joints. Twice. Where you going to go—where you going to go at 4:00 in the morning? You're up. You're wide awake.

I have been known to go out, get drunk, come in, pass out, go to sleep and first shift wake me up and send me home. You know.

So third shift was really getting to be pretty bad with me. No, not healthy at all. But I was losing weight, too. I'd dropped like thirty pounds on third shift where I didn't drop anything on second.

Once I got on second and adjusted to it I was going home at 10:00, doing a little housework, going to bed 11:30, 12:00. Getting up with the kids, sending her off to school. Having some quality time with her. Although I couldn't see her after school. Well, I did a lot at times because I hate to say this, but (pauses) my job lasted no longer than four hours. And we could go and come as we wanted, until just recently when they started getting ready to lay us all off.

They were docking our time and looking at it real hard.

To get it done. They let us know two weeks before time.

You really want to know how I got it this union job? You really want to know?

Okay. There was elections for the alternate committeeman and committeeman. About a month before we got laid off. I had told them I had wanted to run for alternate committee person. Well, Dave Yettaw had gotten in, voted in. So he took his position.

And Dave Yettaw called me up. At work. Told me to come over, he wanted to talk to me.

I said, "Okay, I'll be right over."

Told Marsha, "Run first, I'm going to go over, see Dave Yettaw. I'll do last tonight. And tomorrow I'll do last." Marsha thought, Whoa, she's wonderful. Great friend, you know.

So I went over to Dave Yettaw and he said, "I can't let you run for committeeman." I said, "You have no right to tell me I can't run."

He says, "Well, I'm asking you. I need a unity caucus member in there." I said, "I'm a unity caucus member." He said, "Yeah, but we need somebody with experience."

I said, "Look, I was fired thirteen times in my first ninety days. For almost everything walking in the books. You don't think I have any experience? And I'm still here, working, eleven and a half years later."

He says, "Well, I'll give you something if you don't run." I said, "What can you offer me?"

He said, "I'll get you a standing committee." I said, "What does that consist of?"

He said, "Well, you'll go on conventions all the time. You'll get expenses, you'll have a good time. We don't count on you to give us any information back. All you have to do is fill out this form, come in for an interview and we'll have you your job." Like that.

I said, Fine. I'll give up on that committee person. Right.

Well, I didn't feel I had to be interviewed, right? After this. And he kept saying, I need you to come in for an interview. I said, "Dave, you don't need to interview me. We made a deal." Right. He says, "That's true."

So a friend stood up for me he said, I want to nominate Michele for women's committeeman da-da-da-da-da and I got the post. So, on the first day, he sent us out a letter saying come on in, we want the standing committee bodies to meet.

Well, Mary Stolnaker who's the trustee at Local 599, she said, "Michele, you realize there's three posts open?" I said, "Yeah, I'm running for chairperson."

She said, "Good I'll back you." I said fine. Well, I didn't know that C. L. Anderson, this other woman, had been on the Women's Committee since 1971 and she had been chairperson since 1971. With no opponents, no challenger, right? On a post since 1971.

So I come in there and Jeannie Adams was on there with her the year before. And Doris King, Katie, Mary, and I were the new-comers to the group.

So Jeannie says, "Yes, I'll support Michele." Mary'd talked to her on the way in. Doris, who I'd never knew, she never knew me, said, "Yes, I'll support Michele."

So, C. L. has not done anything for the Women's Committee—not a thing. I read the whole book. I didn't go in there not knowing anything, so I'd read all the books and I found out that she had tried to start programs and never started them, never got anything completed. In 1971 they wanted a fashion show to raise money, you know. There'd never been a fashion show put on since 1971.

Well, at the meeting that Dave Yettaw pulled, before the committees went to meet for the first time, he said he wants the expenses held down, he wants your goals wrote out, submitted to him. Right. Now, I'm writing this down. I'm the only one who's writing this down.

Everybody else is just: Oh, same stuff. They knew.

Well, I wrote it all out. We come into the meeting. And since Mary's trustee, we let her speak first. She says, "I think we better get this meeting on the road. Let's get our chairperson and our vice-chairperson and a secretary." And Mary said, "I nominate Michele Sullivan."

Jeannie Adams said, "I second it. All in favor say, aye." Four ayes, one no. C. L.

So right from that moment I took over. I said, "Okay, now we need a vice-chairperson position filled." I took full control. Full control.

We had a conference coming up within a month. We had to get to the executive board. They wanted to only send two people; we wanted four people sent. We figured out that it was ony $995 because two lost wages and two unemployed people you don't need to pay wages, so it was cheaper that way.

So I said I just want it for the Women's Committee.

He says, "Fine. She got her votes called in, she got it." We were tickled pink.

We went to the Women's Conference in Battle Creek. It's on women and politics, women and the union, lifestyles in the eighties, sexual harassment, you know all the political . . . whatever had to do with women, support, women and children abuse, women's wages being lower than men.

It was very, very good. It was at a real nice hotel in Battle Creek. Nice rooms. Lots of free booze. We got a couple meals free. There was a swimming pool there and a jacuzzi. It was right beside a mall that looked just like a little section of Water Street Pavilion, which was nice.

I'm appointed to this post for three years and I don't get wages, but I get expenses which are not hurting my benefits at all because it's expenses.

So I lucked out there. That was all right. Mileage, $35 a day in food, hotels, I think it's 21 cents a mile. Just expenses.

I don't let 'em pull no crap on me. This was our first initial start. Now being that I'm laid off, I normally need $1,700 a month to live off of. My bills. Not my food, mind you, but my bills. I have one child at home now.

I have two but one's at home.

But I didn't know that I was going to get laid off. Our plant is still open. There's still people with less time working [seniority] than me and that makes me nuts because we were all the same classification. I just found out Wednesday that a friend with a year and a half less than me is in there working in my plant. Where I should be at.

I'm on the Women's Committee and I volunteer for everything. Political, basically. Like I was working on the Bishop Airport Millage Committee. Twenty-four thousand people I figured I talked to in a matter of four weeks.

And I met Dale Kildee, and Mayor Sharp and, well, I met [James] Blanchard [the governor of Michigan] at the AFL-CIO Convention I went to last May. Richard Austin, Owen Bieber.

I'm politically inclined. That's just recently, believe it or not. It's crooked as a hot dog's hind leg, I'll tell you that, and I planned to run for a county commissioner's post because I plan to be in Lansing within the next ten years.

If I don't get back in that shop at all I'm still going to run for school board, county commissioner, something. I'm going to get my foot in the door.

It costs you about $1,000 for campaigning, literature, you know, cards.

Because at this last convention, the attorney general Nancy somebody, she was at our meeting. She give us a nice speech, although I got sick in the middle of it.

But I did listen to her and she said, Start. Do it. Get on the school board, township, clerk, some post to get yourself started. And she said it only took me just a year to get into her first victory.

Yeah, I met quite a few people in that Bishop Airport Millage thing and the AFL-CIO convention.

We at the Women's Committee we wanted to do something for the unemployed worker very, very much because two of us were laid off and there might be three more that might be laid off.

My supervisor had tried to dock me many days when he wasn't docking the black girls that was kissing his ass. Okay.

I know that sounds very prejudiced but that's the way it was. This one gray black chick she would kiss up to him every day. She would be late, later than fifteen minutes, never get docked. Always take two-hour lunches, always leave early. And her and this little group would never get in trouble.

Peggy and I got our jobs done, we got them done, we went Christmas shopping. We were back at 9:00 to punch out, you know, to get ready to go home.

He come by me, he said, "You're docked from 2:30 this afternoon."

I said, "You're crazy."

He took off walking, I started grabbing them pots—the parts we made. I started slinging them at him.

He ran over the stairways over to the next aisle and I'm pitching them over. I'm pitching them right over the lines at him.

I said, "I'll kill you, you SOB, I'll kill you. I'll kill you, honest to god."

He's running and I'm whacking them right behind him. I mean there's a line of baskets and I'm just heaving them at him. And these pots are like fifteen pounds, eighteen pounds, twenty pounds, and I'm just heaving them over there at him.

So he got the committeeman and committeeman come in and said, "What do you think he owes you?"

I said, "For number one, my time. Number two I want an apology, a public apology."

The next day we had to call a meeting. He publicly apologized to me. He didn't dock Peggy now, he only docked me. Okay. He only docked me.

I said, "Now,"—his name's Grossmeyer—I said, "Grossmeyer, now you're really ignorant. You know I come in every day.

You know that January, the first day we're back to work, I tell you the days I want to take off. Don't I?"

He says, "Yeah."

I said, "Now I'm never late, I don't never cheat you, on your parts, I don't never steal no parts from you, and here you treat me like this."

He says, "I'm real sorry."

I said, "Now I want an apology in front of the group."

He said, "Okay. Tomorrow." Tomorrow we went. I got my apology.

But from then on I cheated him.

They do not reward the people that do their jobs, come in every day, are there, tell them when they're going to be off so they can cover them.

Second weekend of September, I'm gone to my party, my four-day party. He's known this. Everybody in General Motors has known this.

They know that if I'm going to be late coming back they can hear from me two days earlier to compensate. I don't leave 'em hanging.

And here they've left me hanging.

Eleven and a half years of my life put in there being good, being the good worker, getting a perfect attendance record, letting them pay me $500 for perfect attendance. Trying not to go on sick leave.

I even fractured my foot walking out of the plant. I went out, fell in a hole, sprained my ankle, tore some ligaments. Waited the whole weekend, go back to work, you know, So I wouldn't get in trouble having another doctor—not a plant doctor—check me out, right, 'cause they got their own. I was off for four weeks I think it was. And they would not pay me workmen's compensation.

They almost refused to pay me sick leave pay. And I was really hurt because I was in there doing the last bit of work getting the system cleaned out, getting everything put away for the long weekend. And they did that to me.

Since about January, I really started to get hostile toward General Motors. The rumors were flying, you know.

But you had committeemen telling you, Well, you won't be affected. But maybe you will get affected. No you won't get affected. One day it was yes, one day it was no, one day it was yes. Back and forth.

I said, I'm not going to worry about it till it gets here. And then two weeks before it got here they laid it down on us. And I was really . . .

I was heartbroken, really.

More emotional you know, because, damn, I worked a long time for them people. I did 'em good. I mean I've always been quality conscious.

When I was in Plant 5, working on inspection, the heat treat was not high enough for these parts. When I was inspecting, there was hairline cracks in them. In the output ring-gear of the transmission. The one that locks it into park.

All parts that go into the car are important to me. But this one was especially important to me because it keeps it in park.

And I called the advisor, I called the foreman over, I said, "Look—we got hairline cracks. I've already went back to heat treat and all the way up through everybody and told them to keep an eye on it."

Which, an inspector's job, didn't say you had to go tell people that something was wrong. Let them figure it out on their own is the old rule.

No, I took the initiative to go back to heat treat, told them the heat is too low, cause I'm getting hairline cracks. I had two tubs full of parts that had hairline cracks in them. And I told them, "Them parts are no good."

He says, "We need them."

I said, "If you need them so bad, you put your name on 'em and you ship them over to 10. Don't put that responsibility on me." I said, "You take my name off that whole tub. 'Cause I put a reject slip on it."

I said, "And if you buy them, you buy them under your name, don't put my name anywhere near them."

He says, "We got to have 'em." They shipped all them bad parts over there. They shipped them bad parts over there.

Count. Count. Count. That's all they worry about is the count.

In the plant I just got laid off from we had egg-shaped pots out of round. They weren't round they were egg shaped.

You can't run them through the machine and get a precise indent or a precise gilman setup. You just can't. Or even a stake. You cannot get a precise stake if the machines are set up for round pots and you get egg shaped.

So they put two of us on this one job where one would hammer and one would pull the parts apart and throw them on the line. The pots were so hard to get apart that you had to have somebody whack the two places and put them on the line.

Well, I was with this little black girl. I'd hear boom-boom. I'd throw two. Boom-boom. Throw two. Boom-boom. Well, she didn't boom-boom and I didn't hear the boom-boom with a hammer. And I put my hand down and she went whack-whack. Got both my hands cut on these pots.

On both my hands, I'm bleeding all over the place, through my gloves and I said, "I've got to go to first aid now. Now I have to go."

He said, "No, you finish your job then you can go."

I said, Fine. Blood all over these pots. All over these parts they're just bloody.

She's going nuts. She don't know what, how I can continue to work and bleed all over these parts.

Yeah, it hurt.

But what am I going to do? I do not want to get fired for not following a direct order. Okay? And that is an automatic fire.

Okay. So, fine, I'll bleed all over your parts.

And when it got over to the gilmans, this poor girl, she saw that the parts had blood on it. She got sick, she puked all over everything and they let her go directly to first aid.

I'm still over there loading parts.

I hurried. I started taking my own parts and banging each other pot to get out of there 'cause I was bleeding so bad.

Granted, they were only superficial cuts. But it was enough blood to make the girl over in gilmans get sick and puke and go to first aid like that.

Their priorities are in the wrong place as far as I'm concerned. They've always been in the wrong place.

I notice that they don't care about quality. Not the people that are working. Some of them. Some of them don't care about it. Very few. Very few in my department didn't care about quality but the majority of us cared.

We were allowed to shut down the machines if the quality wasn't right.

Well, toward the end there, they wouldn't let us shut them down for quality. They would say run them. Period. We need the parts. We need the parts. For the simple reason that if they get the parts they can lay us off sooner than they had anticipated.

They were . . . they're bastards. They don't care about the person. They care about the product regardless . . .

We had the right in our plant if the pots got shipped in and they weren't any good. Now in the beginning, they weren't any good, we shipped the babies back to them. The supplier.

Toward the end, regardless of what garbage come in, we had to build it. We had no say toward the end.

One thing about this plant is they let us have brains. For a change. We didn't want quality work life in our plant cause we already had our own concept. We got it from the Japanese.

It was called "The New Concept."

We got to make decisions, like. You can be there at least fifteen minutes late without losing any pay. And you can leave fifteen minutes early at the end of the shift and you don't lose any pay. We called it cleanup time.

And then lunch—we wanted an hour for lunch. They said, All right fine. Now we got it set down that we started on Sunday night and we got Friday and Saturday night off. On third shift. Which was nice. And I worked third shift eight years. Why? Sixty dollars more a week. Shift premium.

When you get done you're supposed to help other people that don't get done.

Well, I got tired of helping this one group of people that were real lazy. They didn't want to work fast. They didn't want to set their machines up fast. They were piddling around. Taking an hour and a half lunch, two-hour lunch, coming back going, "I'm in the hole. I need help." Right?

The only thing we didn't want to do was exercise. They give us an exercise room. But we didn't want to exercise 'cause we figured, If I walk two and a half hours a day back and forth on these three machines, that's good enough exercise for me.

And I was real upset because I had given my life to General Motors. Literally bought in to this plant. They told me that this plant would be boxed in. I would never get laid off. I would have a job as long as the plant was building torque converters.

Which I felt very happy for. Although if I'd have stayed in the other plant, I'd have had just as good a job as I did before.

They wouldn't supply us with punches, dies and punches that were right. It was bad, I mean it was, it got worse, the closer we got to being laid off. It got worse.

Yeah, I've got forty more weeks and then I'm done. We get benefits, but I've only got eighty SUB-credits left and they use two a week, so I've got forty weeks left. Which'll probably take me to July of next year.

My first thought is I want a job with as condensed learning as I can get, or on-the-job training. To make me $1,700 a week so I don't lose my car. I don't lose my house. I don't lose the possessions I've already acquired.

I would like to be my own boss. But first, the first question I have to ask myself is What does everybody need or want or can consume? And that I have no idea.

I'd like to be my own boss. But I doubt if I'll ever be able to.

Although I know bookkeeping and debits and credits and all that. But. But see, with this Human Resource Center, I can take a job at $5.50 an hour. Human Resources will pay half of my wages and the employer I'm working for only has to pay the other half. The least they'll pay for a job is $5.50 an hour.

If I would have got in the job bank, I could have taken a $3.35 minimum wage job and out of the job banks, they'd have paid me up to what my regular wages were.

But only 149 people can be in the job banks. And you got to know somebody to get in the job bank. It's all who you know or who you don't. (Laughs.)

I don't want to say that too loud, but that's what it is.

I know I'm not really good at public relations. I know that. When I build my own self-confidence up, yeah, I can do it. I could probably relate to people well.

But I've had such a low self-image all my life, you know, you just, you get put down so much.

Like when I first started in the shop. I was a lot bigger than I am now. And I wore my glasses which were Coke bottle bottoms. And every day on the line somebody was tormenting me about my weight or my glasses or my freckles. Just to get you aggravated. Just to get you to quit so you'd be out of their face.

Or throw things at you.

I had this one job. That people would throw doll pins at me. Eight hours, no it was ten hours a day, six days a week. I finally got rebellious and shut the main line down.

That got the supervisors in the area to come over and find out what was wrong.

I said, "You see all these doll pins around me? There are not my job. These are not even near me. What are they doing setting around me? If they end up in your engine, in one of your piston spots and don't come out and you blow an engine, who you going to blame for blowing that $700 engine? If you go in the lifter spots where the lifters go, who's going to be responsible for that? Me?"

I said no. I shut off the line about five times. Finally they took me off the job. Said, Where do you want to go?

In the first plant I worked in, people were denied human rights. Honest to god. If you weren't in cliques, you were definitely . . .

But then I took and went to a different classification and they reduced me out of the plant. Which I was so thankful for because I thought I would be trapped in that plant forever.

I went down to the foundry and it was dirty. I thought I was discriminated against there because I was on inspection and they give me twenty-five extra pounds of equipment to wear for inspection. Which the other inspectors anywhere else, did not have anything but eye protection.

I had steel-toed shoes, the spats, I had leather plastic arm guards. I had an iron apron on, I had the big earmuffs on my ears. I had the great big huge goggles on my face. I had a great big huge respirator and huge gloves. I mean even the women's small gloves at the shop are too big for my hands.

They weren't trying to protect me—they wanted me out. They wanted me to give up.

In fact I eliminated my job.

There was a man behind me with an air chisel. Now this man knew that he had to take off the excess out of where the crankshaft goes on. He knew that he had to remove that excess stock.

And I had a little crayon. When it came out of the shaker, you know, you pour the iron, you let it cool in the casting, and then they go through the shaker and shake all the sand off, right?

He knew that he had to remove this stock, this excess stock.

And I had to set there with a yellow crayon and mark that he knew what his job was. Where to chisel it off at. That was my stupid job.

I felt unproductive. I felt wasted. Useless. How could he not know where it was? Right? The man's been there long enough, he ought to know what to do without somebody telling him.

I wrote up a suggestion. I worked nineteen hours and thirty-six minutes on that line. Then they sent me down to Plant 36, auditing, the plant that I just got out of. Auditing for the foundry. I'm doing the same job that I did before for the same plant. Stupid. Stupid. Right? I thought it was stupid.

So I worked on that one. And then I got laid off again because the foundry was closing.

So I signed up for general plant and they offered me a job in an all man's plant where a woman has never been. Never worked. Never will work is what these guys said. Chaining cars onto railroad.

I had a twenty-five pound ratchet to chain these cars down. They had no coveralls that would fit me. They had no boots that would fit me. No gloves that would fit me. And I was down there six weeks.

We had rain, we had snow, we had sleet, we had sunshine. We had every existing weather condition. In these six weeks.

I went in there with Ernie. Ernie and I have almost the same identical seniority. Although he was a man, he got accepted right away. I mean totally. He was playing cards with them. They wouldn't let me play cards with them on our breaks. They totally outcasted me.

I come into work, I'd have to wait for every one of them to get changed, then go in and change. My bathroom was three buildings over. My shower was three buildings over.

They got me coveralls finally. Size 65 or something, right? So the crotch is down to my knees. I got 'em rolled up, got the sleeves rolled up, and the damn armpits way down here at my wrist. They got me the smallest size boots they got, which was size twelve.

I had my steel-toed boots on inside these boots. Okay?

Now, I'm on my knees eight hours a day. My knees swell up. It was like almost an arthritic condition. I couldn't walk. I was in pain. They sent me three buildings over the other way to go to the first aid.

They told me no more kneeling. Great. So they give me a job I can't remember the name of it, some stupid off-the-wall name.

You'd get in there in the morning and you'd go out and get yourself a car. I always grabbed a big old Park Avenue with the CB, AM/FM stereo in it. And you sleep until 9:30 in the morning. Shift starts at 6:00 but you don't have to start until 9:30 in the morning.

Then all of a sudden here comes this bus. You all jump in there with the bus, you got a pencil, rubber bands, stapler, and cards. You have to run out of that van, jump in the car, make sure the number's right. You take the car, back it up, and you run and you drive it up on these railroad cars in line. You jump out, you run down, you run back in the van and they haul you back out and you do the same thing over. You have to do fifteen railroad cars.

Now, I'd never been the first driver of a lead-off car. Never. They said, "You're lead-off this time." They had removed one of the pallets between the railroad cards. They said, "Okay, go!" I mean you got to go! I mean if you don't drive fast, you're going to get everybody ticked off at you.

So, I'm buzzing through this railroad car and I didn't notice that this one was off and I went boom, tore the catalytic converter off this car. And it's going bum-bum-bum. Real loud.

The guys get out of the cars, said, "Well, why didn't you see that wasn't there?" I said, "Hey, it's always been there before when I'm behind you."

So, one of them goes and tells the advisor, well, they were called foremens then. Goes tells the foreman that I had wrecked a car.

Right?

Well, by this time a few of them had realized that they had went to school with me. And that they better take care of me because I'm going to be at their class reunions, I'm going to really make them feel bad, you know. I'm going to get my revenge if nothing else.

Well, they took the catalytic converter, threw it underneath the train, pushed my car back up there, put the ramp there, and I parked it. By the time this guy got back.

So out comes the supervisor with his little violation pad. I'm going to write you up for destruction of property. I'm giving you x amount of days off. I said, "You better get me the committeeman."

He says, "You have no committeeman. You're the only woman that works here." I have no committeeman. I said, "Wait a minute, I paid my damn union dues, you're not going to do this to me." I said, "You get me my committeeman or so help me God, I'll get Labor Relations on your ass."

He said, "I guess you can do that." I said, "You know I can do that. You ain't got no stupid girl here."

Then the committeeman shows up three days later, but I'm not out on the street. I'm in there with this paperwork on me. So committeeman shows up, I said, "Look, I know my rights, I know I was set up, I know this is the way it was. I'd never drove lead-off before," I said I believe I was set up.

He says, "How can you say that about these men? I've worked with them, I've been committeeman for them."

I said, "I don't care what you've been for these men. Now you've got me underneath your jurisdiction. Now you better take care of me, 'cause if you don't I'm going up to the president of the local."

He said, "Okay, I'll go get it ripped up."

This one guy come in drunk. And he took a nice pretty yellow Buick, hit a nice patch and wrapped it around a telephone pole. Ran away from the car.

Somebody went and told the supervisor that it was me—they saw me getting out of this car. Down comes the supervisor.

Chewing me up. I said, "Wait a minute. I'm over in D-7 right now. I did not have anything to do with it."

He said, "That ain't what I heard."

I said, "Well, I don't care what you heard. I'm telling you somebody set me up. If you don't like it, you just do what you got to do and I'll do what I got to do."

He said, "Well, I see that you didn't do it."

I said, "Well, thank you very much."

Fine.

A van got stolen. The one that you take the drivers around in. Now these six guys had gotten drunk a bunch, took this van and there was a low cement bridge. They hit it, they tore the roof off of the van. Some teeth were loose. Somebody got a broken arm. Somebody got hit on the head. There was other injuries that you could visually see.

Guess who got blamed for that one? Me.

I said, "What time did this happen?"

Well, I happened to be somewhere where I was seen, thank God. By other Buick workers, right?

I had to go get these people, bring them down to my plant, and prove that I was somewhere else when this happened.

Finally, we all had a break at the same time because the line had broke down over in final assembly, so we all had a break. We were all sitting up in the break room.

I come up in that room, I said, "Look, you SOBs," I said, "You son-of-a-bitches, you have done nothing but torment me, hide my shit on me. There's only been four of you people in this whole room that cared anything about me being a human being. I tell you what, the next time any you SOBs fuck with me I'm going to blow your shit away."

From that time they never did anything wrong with me. They let me play in their card games with them. They let me get in on their little raffles. Anytime anybody went out to eat, I was always asked, Do you want anything to eat when we go out? I had to show them men that I was just as tough as they were. And I could get into their shit.

I wasn't going to let them chew me up. I chewed them up. I mean I was real mean to them.

Finally, they offered me back my job in Plant 81. I went right back to the same job. Same pay raise. I been there ever since until August 7th.

I'd been in the same, almost every plant I've went into, I've had bullshit given out. Every time. Like when I went to Plant 5.

There was only one other woman in the whole plant with me.

Now, Louise and I got along really good. She was over in this department, I was in this department. But yet, we seen each other and the minute I seen another woman I said," Hi! how are you? How are you?" You know, get friendly with her.

Well, she had already made friends with the guys because she had more seniority than most of the men in there in her department. But yet when she first come in the department with the old timers, they give her the same bullshit.

She told me, "Don't take no bullshit off these boys. Don't take no bullshit. The minute you let 'em walk over you, that's it. You're going to be walked on."

I said, Okay, thanks for the, you know. The warning.

After that it was all right.

I was not a great swearer before I went into that shop. Now, I'm a super good swearer. I mean it goes with the territory. And there's only one rule that I've followed: You never date anybody that you work with. And I broke my rule once, ended up marrying him and he left me for another woman. So.

I have kept that rule. I try not to go out with anybody that works at Buick. But if they work in my plant—no way. Not where I have to see them.

Time in the shop is funny. They never change. No, you get in a rut. And you're like in suspended animation when you're in the shop. Because everything's so repetitious, everything's . . .

When I was working seven days a week, twelve hours a day, in Plant 36, I would go in and I would do my job, take my breaks and I would go home, go to bed, get up, go back to work, take my breaks, go home. And I was stuck in that time frame. And I never got out of it.

But I enjoyed that. I felt very productive when I was working at Buick. I feel less productive now. Than I ever did.

Because I could see my work. When I was in the shop, I could see that I was a productive human being in this world. But since I've been laid off . . .

Well, see, in this "New Concept" thing they said, Well, whenever you're done, go help somebody else. Right? Well, I would be in pumps department and I would go to another department and I would help my friend get their job done. Granted, it was my friend, but I was still under the concept.

And I would have advisors come by, "What are you doing? Why aren't you in your department? Why aren't you doing your job?" "I'm done, I'm helping someone else, I have 'The New Concept' under my belt." And they'd say, "Oh, wonderful, you know this person down here, they need a little." I said, "I don't know this person, I can't help them. I want to help my friend here." Granted, it was selfish, but I didn't want to help somebody else because then they'd use me up. Want me to come down every day.

I want to be helpful, but I don't want to be used, being helpful. And if a person was piddling around, shucking and jiving, talking, not doing his job, see, I don't feel they deserve my help.

This other guy said, "I gotta' go to the bathroom." I said, "Okay. I'll watch your job, go to the bathroom." He was gone two hours to the bathroom. I said, "You used me up, buddy. You used me up, don't ask me to help you again." You know.

I've got some extra skills. Like I've taken two welding classes. I wanted to get on trades as a welder. And then I found out I can wear contacts and I didn't want to be a welder anymore because you can't wear contacts, right? And I hate my Coke bottle bottom glasses, right?

In my two welding classes I used a little artistic initiative. And my brother-in-law, he likes sailboats. So I heated the metal, soddered a sailboat and the waves and the sun and the clouds and the birds on it, on both sides.

And I heated it to where the metal changed colors so it was sort of copperish colored. I changed the color of the metal, I grinded it, I polished it, made it real smooth, and I give it to him for Christmas and he liked it.

Then I took a whole bunch of weaves, I learned this new cutting machine, and I cut out all kinds of hearts sizes. It was real thin metal and I made charms out of them.

Yeah, I love machinery. I like anything mechanical. I always have.

They said I could be in auto repair body. But that isn't what I want to be. In this job that I've had for the last six years, I dress good, I dress neatly to go in. I don't get dirty. I have coordinating outfits.

I've gotten into a routine where I don't like to get dirty. And I don't like to wear coveralls.

But now if I go into politics, I'm going to have to spend an arm and a leg to get the right clothes. I can spend $250, have eight or nine outfits off of $250 bucks. Or putting on makeup. I've just now got it down pat. I finally got rid of all the straight long hair and got to something that all I have to do is turn my head over, blow my hair dry, and go.

Another thing I'd really like to do is manicures, putting on, doing nails, porcelain nails.

This girl at the shop, an electrician, she took a course doing nails. And I said, "Well, I'll come over and have my nails porcelained," right? Well, her nails started breaking because of her job. I said, "Well, I'll do it for you, I've been watching you enough."

So I ended up doing her hands better than she was doing my hands and she had the license.

This is my wildest dream.

I would like to get a styling—I don't want to be a cosmetologist. I want to become a stylist. With nails, you know, with doing the nails, your porcelain, the designs on the nails and stuff.

Then I want to get a big bus with four chairs, four dryers, two wash basins, a manicurist's spot with a water holder, and I want to go into like the residential areas, park my bus and have people walk out of their house into my bus, have another girl or maybe another two girls working with me, and drive my bus around and do things in the communities.

Like there's old folks. Granted now-a-days, they've got the walk-ins. But if you pull up in a subdivision and you're setting on the corner and this old woman, she hasn't been out in awhile because she's afraid to go out—I could do her. Or a man. I want to do unisex. Come out, get your hair done. That's what I want to do. That's my wildest dream.

And it would take about $25,000 to get the bus with the heater with the water supply I would need. That. And my license and my business license and all the regulations you got to go through. That's what I would like to do. That's my wildest dream.

Although (sighs) I happened to mention it to my friend and her husband. And this other girl. We were sitting there and Mary wants to open a bathroom boutique, coordinate your bathroom.

Stan says, "Join Mary and you girls can put your money together and you girls can do this."

I said, "No way," and I told them about the bus.

He said, "That's about the stupidest idea I ever heard of. Nobody will be wanting, nobody will be coming to your bus to get their hair done and nails done."

And then this other girl, she said, "That's really a stupid idea."

And within a matter of minutes I was shot down so low that I didn't open my mouth again the whole day I was so despondent. But that to me sounds really inventive. Nobody else has done it. Nobody else will ever do it.

There's no overhead with a bus. I mean, if you put in $5 worth of gas, you can go to a subdivision and maybe get eight, ten people. Granted, my hairdos are going to cost, I'm going to style your hair. If I'm not going to just basic set it, I can make some money.

See, if I was living near Ann Arbor, I would be doing punk hairdos. I like punk rockers.

That's one of my wildest dreams, but it takes about a year. If I wanted the investment, I could take my Golden Handshake and go out with about a $18,000, but you know, but if I ever do go back to the shop, I'm going to save to go somewhere else.

If I get four and a half or three and a half more years in the shop I will be saving my money. I already told my daughter, I said,

"Look, if I ever do get called back to the shop, we are not going to live like we did."

We are going to pay the car payment and we are going to pay the house payment and we are not buying anything on installment again. Ever.

I ripped up, I cut up all my credit cards except one. And that's my gas one.

I told here, "When we get 'em all paid off, that's it. No more."

Oh, I know where all my money went. 'Cause I'm the only one that made out the bills. I'm the only one that signed the IOUs.

It was me.

I was going from an overtime overtime job to a forty-hour-a-week job. I knew that. I signed into 81 for the forty hours. I wanted the forty hours. I wanted the weekends free, which I'd never had in eight years.

Others, they want overtime. I never did. When I bought into that plant, I wanted the forty hours a week. I wanted it. These other people were forced on it. And now that they got their time in the shop and got groups and whatever, they start forcing the ones that have been in there since jump street out, you know. And they don't care about what we were taught in our original concept. Because they only had an eight hour class of it.

The first ones had a week. Like Sandy and Mac, my friends, they went to the week-long ones. And they told me all the garbage that they went through. Like putting names on their foreheads. They can't see what it is, like, one of them said, "This is an idiot." "This is a slob." "This is a creep." "This is a moron." And then how you would talk to 'em, react accordingly.

I sat in the classes for three days. And listened to all their mumbo-jumbo. One thing they did teach me was to listen. Which I'd never listened before.

I try. I try every day at work when somebody was talking to me, I was listening to them. We were put face-to-face and you had to speak for two and a half minutes straight at the person and then when that person was done, then you had to talk two and a half minutes straight to that person. You had to look in their eyes, make eye contact. You had to make direct contact you couldn't talk or look anywhere else except at this person for two and a half minutes. That was the training we had. But we had to do it over and over and over again until everybody in orientation class got it down pat.

The more I'm talking to people, the more I realize that I do have personal interraction skills, I guess, which I never thought talking to somebody was personally interacting. Oh, is that it? Okay. (Laughs.)

Well, like, with this rap session that's coming up, Mary initiated it. I took over and said, "Well, I think we need a credit counselor there."

I'm going, "Hey, I got laid off at the shop, I got three more years to pay on most of my stuff. What do I do now?"

And Mary's going, "What do we need credit counseling in here for?" I said, "I tell you what, I'm an unemployed worker and I'm not the only john in the bag out here. I'm telling you that there are people out there wondering what to do about their credit. Before it gets too bad."

And the counselor told me right off the top, Don't pay anybody that doesn't have collateral behind their bills. Anybody who can't take something away. So I have yet to pay Genesee Merchants Bank $139.76. You can eventually work into credit counselor where they'll pay x amount of dollars, where it won't take your whole check.

Well, I worked on my own and I got my car payment down from $115.79 a week down to $360 a month. Okay? I can handle $360 for a car payment, but I can never go back to having my life and disability insurance put back on it.

If I go back [to the shop], I'm going to trade my little car in and I'm going to get me another identical car like it on a two-year investment and pay my $500 a month and get it out of my way in two years.

And then Mary said, "Oh, no. I don't like somebody coming in talking about training programs." And I said, "Wait a minute, wait. This is real life, girl you've got to realize it." I said, Let me take and put a little emphasis on this. Okay.

Well, the Swan Ice Cream Factory just opened up in Clio and I'm thinking about going out there and applying for the maintenance part of it see, because I've got all this experience. I had to repair my own machine, see, 'cause I was setup. Quality operator means setup.

And it's right down the road from me; I can walk it if nothing else. Or ride a bicycle.

But, I think, Now you better get some training. You better find another job. You better maintain. Don't get suicidal. Don't cry, don't be depressed. Because tomorrow is another day. It's got to get better. By all odds tomorrow should be better than today.

It's definitely devastating. But you can't let it whip you. You've got to go on.

And don't bottle up inside you. Talk to your clergyman or reverend or rabbi or priest or whatever. Talk to somebody about it. Don't let it eat you up. 'Cause if you let it eat you up, you're going to be in worse shape than you were.

Try and find a solution. Use every available resource you can find and use. Go back to school, get more training.

I try to have an angle on everything is what my motto is. I try to have an angle. I've done some dark angles to get somewhere, I've used blackmail. I have. Because if I find out something about somebody, I'll hold it instead of telling it. I'll keep it for my own value.

In the plant, you've got to be deceptive. I've never lied, though. I don't like to lie. I don't like to lie to anybody. Because I've got such a bad memory.

So I don't tell lies. I'm very truthful. I'll always be very truthful. That's one thing I can say that's good in my favor.

Sanford

David and Lois Marie Sanford, both in their mid-forties, were interviewed together. Dave had worked at Buick Manufacturing for twenty-one years, and he and his wife experienced the life-style transition together.

The couple had three children between them from previous marriages and were building a successful life together when the career change occurred.

Dave Sanford had quit the shop instead of waiting for the coming layoff before being hired as a free-lance reporter for the Flint Journal.

Lois went out on assignments with him and began using first her photography and then her writing skills. Eventually, she reported stories under her own name.

Dave's slick black hair and blue eyes make him look younger than his years. Lois looks like a young school girl, with brown hair and quick brown eyes that are partially hidden behind glasses. Both are articulate, bright, and obviously enjoy each other's company.

LOIS: Well, it had started out I knew he wasn't happy where he was. And we discussed him transferring to the Saturn plant. But we knew that was a long time off.

DAVE: We didn't know how long off.

LOIS: We even went so far as picking up real estate brochures and stuff. To figure out some possibilities. Then it just got to the point where it was getting worse and worse and worse.

Suddenly he was getting sick, which he'd never been a day in his life. He'd go to work two or three nights. He'd miss two or three nights. Then he missed a week.

I finally told him to think about it. We laid up there talking about it. He said, "I just can't handle this anymore." And I said, "Okay, how about a transfer within the plant? Get out of your department." He put in for one but it was: Well, maybe, but. It was going to be three months before that could happen.

DAVE: At the time there weren't any openings.

LOIS: So he was getting worse and worse. He'd come home and couldn't sleep.

DAVE: And that's not me. I guess in a way I couldn't wait for the plant to close, because I just ran out of steam.

LOIS: Emotional steam.

DAVE: Okay. There's this constant struggle to try and keep things going [in the plant]. And there was a lot of trouble with the employees and management at the time who just wanted to shut everything down.

They just didn't want to do their job. You know, if something broke down, they'd say, "That's great. Now we can just sit around." And get overtime for it, just sitting around.

LOIS: *Why should we work our butts off now if we can wait and get overtime?*

DAVE: Right. And for a while I'd been coordinator which meant I was kind of in charge of what was going on in that area. And I kept the place running. And there were two guys who just hated that. They didn't want things running.

They said, "You're ruining our overtime. You're helping put people out of work." You know, by doing your job.

And the tension got bad. And I took a week off. During that week I was gone, they removed me as coordinator. So they elected one of these guys who didn't want to do anything. And from then on he was steadily on my butt. "Ah, we don't want you to run—quit running all these parts. You're running twice as many parts as anyone else. We don't want you to do this."

And I got angry with them. And finally, the last straw. I was battling with the parts line all night. I ran seven hundred parts—about half of what I should have run—by getting it fixed every fifteen or twenty minutes.

And at the end of that shift I was taking counts on all the machines and I came over to number 7 and it only had 135 parts on it. I said "What's wrong with number 7? Is it down?" And they said no, the gal that was running it had to go back there and unplug it every fifteen minutes so I told her she didn't have to unplug that conveyer, we'll just shut the machine down.

So she shut the machine down and just walked around the plant for seven hours while I'm fighting with this one over here.

And at that point I just said, What's the use? You know, you're trying to bust your butt to do a job and the guy next to you is trying to screw it up.

I just hate inefficiency and to me that's practically saying to the Japanese, "Just come in and take over the place." If we're going to run that badly we might as well quit.

The problem is that everybody's caught inside a bullshit system. A system that financially rewards the inefficiency and ineffectiveness of the workers.

You'll make more money and you're more sure of your job, most people feel, at least in the short time, if you don't put out as many parts. If you get too efficient, when they've got enough cars they'll lay you off. If you get too efficient you don't get more Saturdays [overtime].

Look at Factory 86. For years they made seventy-five percent of their production on Thursday, Friday and Saturday. Monday, Tuesday and Wednesday night they never made anything. But they posted they were going to work overtime on Saturday and so everyone knew they were going to make overtime.

You know, it's true, a lot of people say, "Well, look, I can't make enough on five days a week. I want overtime."

So they get overtime for not doing their job on straight time so that you have to have the overtime to do the job.

When we used to run a lot of parts wrong and they needed to be repaired, we couldn't get people to repair them. You'd get two or three guys during regular hours and ask them and they'd say, "Hey, we're not going to do this now, this is our overtime money."

You've got a bunch of people figuring out what they have to do to get by.

Some are like that already, but another part of it is that they don't really identify that their activities are going to affect General Motors and Buick. You know, they don't think the effectiveness of the large company has anything to do with their inefficiency. They don't believe one guy, on one part, is going to affect anything.

Lois: I have to back up and tell you the story about the night he couldn't go in.

We were just living together at the time. He had left for work and was back home. I'd been sick. I thought he was coming back home because he was worried about me. And he pulled up in the driveway, you know, and he just didn't come in the house.

And finally I went outside and he was leaning up against the car. And I said, "Honey, aren't you going to come in?" And he said, "I don't know. Do I still have a home?"

Because he knew he couldn't go back to work.

He felt like he was giving the kids and I the world. Because we'd been on welfare almost ever since the kids were born. And we had spent a fantastic summer running here and running there. My welfare was paying the bills and we were blowing his checks.

Dave: Not really.

Lois: Pretty much.

Dave: There were a lot of things that were needed.

Lois: And cripes, we got a washer [raises her eyebrows in surprise, signalling it was the first time she had owned her own]. And he fixed my van for me and we took the kids to Mackinac and . . . and neat things, you know. And he really felt bad because then leaving the plant meant we weren't going to have those things.

Dave: I quit with no idea in the world what I was going to do. I quit October 13, 1985. Married July 15, 1985. So we were fairly new married when this happened.

I didn't decide to quit. I couldn't hack it. I got very involved in the new way of running the shop, [Quality of Work Life, which stresses quality] and trying to make it run efficiently and so forth. And there's an awful lot of opposition to it.

I would say probably seventy-five percent of the people in the shop are opposed to trying to do the job better. They're convinced it's going to cost them money. It's going to cost them jobs. And they're against it.

I got real irritated about it. I'd been fighting with them for five or six years. Two other times I'd worked on ways of getting a job, establishing myself and getting out but that didn't work. I don't want to go into all the details on it.

And finally, one day I drove into the parking lot and I couldn't get out of the car. I just literally could not get out of the car. I couldn't go in there and face all that bullshit anymore.

And it's going to sound like I'm talking bad about the company, and it really wasn't the company. It was some fellow employees as much as anything else. People who just didn't want to do their job and I was tired of it.

I guess I'm a perfectionist in some ways. I think when you do something you ought to do it right for as long as you can.

I didn't have a job. So [sighs], for about a month I tried to apply for a leave and evidently it was turned down.

And then they put me down as a voluntary quit 'cause I couldn't come to work.

I didn't figure out another job. It was sudden. I didn't know I was going to quit.

The reporting started with a book. I wrote a book about the shop. I took the book in and showed it to Ken Palmer who was the [Flint] *Journal* labor writer at the time. And we got to talking about it and I happened to mention that I saw Al Wilhelm there and I thought he was retired. And he said, "Oh, no, he's the Metro Editor, he's my bosses' boss."

So I went in and talked to him about the book and he gave me some helpful suggestions. He thought of publishing it for awhile. Everyone was for it but Peloquin [editor of the Flint *Journal*].

Anyway, I just happened to mention to him, I said, "If you need a cub reporter, I'm really out of work and I'm desperate. And he said, "Oh, well, we always need stringers who can write and I can see by the book, you can write. So come on."

And he told me to come in and talk to Mike Riha, who was running the stringers then. I talked to him and Mike wasn't very enthusiastic, I must say.

I didn't know very much about how to write a newspaper story. And when I wrote the first one I didn't realize that you're only supposed to cover one subject per story. I put too much information in.

So he [Riha] told me to come in and talk to John Davis who was the night editor then. And John showed me how to write a story.

That was February of 1986.

It was tough from October to February. I tried for a number of jobs in the meanwhile and every place I went they said, "You have twenty-one years in at Buick and now you're looking for this job? You have three years of a college education?" They wouldn't even talk to me.

I once talked to a security outfit that wanted telephone solicitors. (Lower, rougher.) They wouldn't even talk to me. Too much education. Dominos Pizza was willing to "consider" me. They would rather have someone that they thought would stay there longer.

Another thing is that usually when you find someone who's lost a job in the shop after twenty-one years, they're an alcoholic. Or a drug abuser. Or they've committed a crime. You don't lose a job with twenty-one years service very easily. (Laughs uneasily.)

People don't want to hire you if you've worked for General Motors for a long period of time and then left. They wonder why. They wonder what's happened.

Anyway, this [reporting] did not make us much money. The first months we were making like $200, $300.

We had talked to friends who I had helped buy their place up in Tuscola County and they had ten acres. They said, Fine, we'll sell you an acre. And we moved the mobile home up there.

Since we were moving to that area, I talked to Al and he said, "That's great, we need somebody to cover that area. We need to get back into that. We haven't done it for years." So then, we kept building up our area coverage.

Right now, I cover parts of four counties. We have Marathon Township, Lapeer County, several areas that we cover in Tuscola County, Forest and Thetford Township, Birch Run Township and Saginaw Township.

If there's nothing going on in one place, generally, there's something going on someplace else. The territory in Lapeer and Genesee County we just got. And that's what put us up to the income where we don't need ADC to supplement our income anymore.

I'll say this. It was scary. And I'll tell you this. And I don't even want this in the book. But there was twice—twice that there was a pistol on the bed between us. And we were saying, Now, is it time to shoot ourselves? Or do we really keep on trying to do this?

LOIS: His GM stock paid for the septic system and the trailer move itself and a lot of things that without that stock to sell we couldn't have done. Several times we almost lost the car.

DAVE: Then I got $1,500 back from my last year's income tax return. Because I had not worked for the last four months. We had

$3,000 and that put the place in. That, and a loan from a personal friend. We had $3,000 to work with.

Lois: And that didn't go far, especially when you're talking septic systems and moving trailers fifty miles.

Dave: Well, that did pay . . . I think we paid $3,200 for all the work we had to do to get that place ready.

But what happens is ADC doesn't pay you enough to live on. And every nickel or dime . . . you never realize. Three kids in school. Kids' pictures come along. Eighteen dollars apiece for three kids' pictures.

Lois: Let's say the kid needs basketball shoes, or whatever, you know.

Dave: Ah (laughs) the money I made in the shop—it just vanished. So that's why I ended up having to borrow from friends. The money just vanished.

We went last winter with no water. We carried water from the neighbor's for drinking. We carried water from the pond for flushing toilets.

Lois: We took showers in the pond.

Dave: The money vanished.

This spring we got the water system hooked up—I think in April. So the house is essentially finished. We haven't had our final inspection yet. Some silly things yet, like tie-downs.

It's a mobile home. A fourteen by seventy [foot] mobile home. It's hers, not mine.

Lois: Well . . . I was with another guy. I was just divorced. So I couldn't get any credit. So Dave signed for it and sold it to me on land contract and two years later moved into it. (Laughs.)

ADC accepts land contract on mobile homes all the time.

Dave: By the time I'd been writing for two or three months, I was saying things like, Gee, I'm going to hate to have to quit this, but sooner or later I'm going to bump into a job that pays . . .

Lois: . . . pays me something . . .

DAVE: . . . pays me fifteen or twenty thousand a year. I'm going to have to quit this but I love it! And I wish I could get a chance to do it all the time. Well, now I guess I do. The money's finally worked out.

LOIS: And at that time he had thought about going back into the shop and he was trying to figure out how he could; work at the shop and still keep the newspaper job.

But I said, "Hey, wait a minute. Somewhere in there, there's got to be time for us, too. For me and the kids." And I said, "If you're going to be going to cover [school board, township] meetings every night and working five days a week, where are you going to find time for us?"

DAVE: But now we're making near what we should.

My advice for anyone going through this is: Plan, plan—go on with your life with the income you've got coming in. Don't wait for miracles to happen. They won't.

Don't wait to get a job. Plan: How am I going to live for the next five years on the income I've got coming in?

Whether it's welfare or unemployment or whatever. You know, how am I going to have a house that I can pay for? How am I going to be able to pay for my kids' school clothes? Because we had to do that. We had to get out of the trailer park where we were at. The rent was too high. If we'd have stayed there we were never going to be able to pay it. We would have had to get $30, $50 a month from somebody just to pay that.

We had to get out of there. And we did. We had to find something that we could pay for. Something that we could do to get money. In fact, I'm not sure that some of the things we did were exactly legal.

LOIS: Like we returned things for money. (Laughs.)

DAVE: But you do what you have to do.

Church

Judith Church, a spiritely, fortyish woman, had worked at Buick for more than ten years. She and her husband, an insurance broker, have five children, ranging in age from fifteen to twenty-five.

It was obvious from a Local 599 meeting that she has no problem speaking up or asking questions.

She has not yet secured employment, but is beginning to consider different training programs.

I have five children, one born in just the last few months.

We have children who have married real young. Two of them have been married in the last year. But we have one that's just turned fifteen at home and another one that was completely burned out in a fire in her apartment. She lost everything and she's twenty-three. And she's under our roof and trying to be self-supporting and going back to college and holding down a full-time job and going down to apply to that place in Rochester to try to have some medical coverage because we can't carry it on her anymore.

I graduated from a private school at seventeen, was already lined up to go with United Airlines. Already been interviewed, already taken French in college while I was a senior in high school.

And then along came the guy in the white shining armor. (Laughs.) And five children later . . . I'd stayed home to raise the five kids for about fourteen years. Then I was twenty-nine and realizing when my daughter was two, that hey, our finances had bottomed out. My husband, he'd hurt his back years ago, his job was bringing in $72 a week. ADC was going to give me more money than he was able to bring in. About eleven years ago. That wasn't good, then, with five children.

Things had been the pits. Four of us had been in the hospital, through no fault of our own. Things were real bad. So it took me nine months through MESC, but I chose to go to work at Buick, after seeing what I was going to make on ADC.

The joke with my brother was, if you have to leave five children—and you work where it's morally, legally and ethically possible—get the highest pay because you're selling your time.

So I chose to go to work at Buick.

I had worked before part-time as a salesperson. But pretty much, it was just stay home and taking care of five children.

My husband had quit Buick after about five and a half years with a real good work record. Enough to be a foreman, taking classes for skilled trades. And then decided he was bored with it and quit. With my fourth child on the way. It was fun.

His father had been an electrician at Buick before him. My grandpa had forty-two years in at Buick. We come from a long line, both of us, of people that work for GM in this town.

So I worked for them almost eleven years. I went on QC (Quality Control) after an injury on my hand at Buick.

And QC flows Buick-wide. So I got a grand tour of Buick.

Plant 5, 10, 4, 40, 12, Big 12, Little 12, 31, 36. Nine plants because every time there was a layoff or change in seniority list, a cutback, we were the bottom two on the list. So we'd have to go. If there was a reduction in force in plant 36 or plant 10 as there was once, of nine people Shirley and I lost the job and had to hire in at a different plant. So we did a lot of inspecting in a lot of places.

It was interesting. But I finally got tired of it.

I had to work standing inside a press that would match a hood and I'm wondering if I'm going to get mashed, 'cause they're tearing the presses down around me. And they're old and anti-quated and ready to go out the door and I'm climbing inside to get a speck of dust.

It's been a lot of interesting jobs.

I was injured on the line in Plant 4 and 40 when I first hired in at Buick Final Assembly. I was about one of the first women down in the pit. We were handling airguns with a ninety-pound torque. Larry England was my foreman.

It was a big joke to him that I should happen to say that I was in pain. I was a new employee and I stayed in the pit.

The final result was that I had carpal tendon injury and my hand tore up. He said, "Well, it was only because it was a woman."

The two men, Mike and George who went in the pit right

after me also tore up their hands. Finally, the job was changed. The guns were changed.

And then it was out of the pit and on to QC after the operation. And, as I said, I had a grand tour of Buick because of the low seniority.

I went off QC and was barely holding on with my seniority and was laid off from Plant 36. I was at Buick City at Final Assembly the last day we shut down. I didn't take what turned out to be an almost nine month layoff for a lot of people.

Forty-eight hours before we went out that door, they gave the truck drivers and the QC people the option to not take the layoff. I didn't take the layoff because there was no way we could ever get our jobs because the cutbacks would be so drastic in those areas.

Two hundred eighty-some of us, and only eleven chose to not take the layoff but go to work. And I hired in immediately to general plant. Never did take that layoff from Buick City.

I was working at General Plant at Plant 36 until my seniority wouldn't hold that anymore. Our whole line was shut down. Instead of going to the D line, because of restrictions on my hands, I left Plant 36 and was able to hire immediately back to Plant 5 back where I had been for years at one point. I'd been at Plant 5 the most. It kind of felt like it was my home plant.

I didn't take a long layoff at Plant 36 either. My idea had always been: I want to work.

The last time I was off I went back to work at Final Assembly, went off QC.

I was put on two big massive airguns and it wasn't too long before my other hand was torn up. They were the two heaviest guns on the line. They already knew I had had one hand operated on but nobody really seemed to care. So. And then that hand was operated on, my right hand.

I left because of the operation, because I thought this is no place for me. I and air guns do not make it. Then back on to QC after that operation and then, those last few hours before we were out for months at Buick City.

I had an option again to work [instead of taking a layoff] as a job setter in Plant 5. Like I said, I kind of half-felt it had been my home plant. I'd learned eleven different inspecting jobs and I started on the ITW's [type of engine] when again, back before, I couldn't hold that plant as being QC.

So I went back into Plant 5 but this time I was given the option to be a job setter and I took the training and went on setup on a machine floor. That's where I was finally laid off from. From Plant 5 Hydromatic Division.

Because, as a typical woman, we're likely to get our hands on as much gossip as we can, I knew it was coming. I had anticipated it from the previous December. But *nobody* would give you anything definite.

I choose to go to Dewey Clark and ask to see the seniority list. See where I was at. I chose to talk to JR, John Rogers, my committeeman. Bug the poor man, tease him, Okay, John, fill me in, where we at?

And so, I had an idea what was coming.

Then it was a matter of wondering when the higher pay classification, or the boxed jobs would be broken open. And as soon as that happened I was out of the plant. Which was Thanksgiving week of '87.

I liked the job that I was on, I was proud of it. I was running at one time—you'll laugh—it was wrong, it's illegal, but our production, and our quality was good. At one point I was doubling up with a partner and running frantically, you might say, twenty machines.

We didn't have to. We did it for just a short period of time.

Once they were set up, changes were done, the machines were warmed up, things were taken care of. We could then help cover each other's machines.

But at one point it was twenty-five machines and they took five of them away and put them in another department. But basically, I was responsible for running in the end, ten machines. Which are rigid hobbers, they're a hobbing operation which cuts the gears.

How would you describe it? Job setter on a machine floor on a hob. Okay?

Each machining operation was different as a job setter on the hobs. They're planetary gears. We were cutting the small gears on the planetary system, not the sun gears. The small gears that would rotate on the outside. There's four of them. Okay, we're cutting those from fourteen to sixteen thousand a night. Okay, they're off those machines and we got it down to around an average of twenty-three seconds per pinion of cutting the gears.

This is close to one final machining process, where you take out a blank rod, you've cut it like cinnamon rolls on a roll, you punch the hole into it, you've made the gear, you've polished that gear, you've sent it over and now we're cutting the teeth.

The adjustment we made would adjust the width of the gear, of the tooth on the gear.

My last day worked was the day before Thanksgiving. It was real interesting because they gave us the week before that off. So, I was laid off for the week before. They kept sucking up my unemployment benefits so that I only had eighteen unemployment credits left out of twenty-six weeks when I went out that door.

There was no notice given. It was just an assumption: Judy, you're going to get it soon. So, if I wasn't nosy, if I didn't keep with my foot in the door, I might not have known so soon.

It had been a thought for six months that the money is going away and the bills aren't. (Laughs nervously.)

February, January last year, we put the house on the market for sale. See, I thought a year ago Christmas I might get it. So, from January to July we had the house up on the market for sale and tried to move the house.

For three and a half months previous, before I actually got the layoff, I was trying to sell the car. I hadn't been able to move the house. We had an '86 car just before we found out I might lose my job. And we still owe like $14,000, which wasn't outrageous. At that point my husband was making good money and so was I.

We knew we had $15,000 into the house. We put it on the market at $5,000 less than we paid for it and it still didn't move. We tried that last January. We realized that the mileage we'd run up on the car was preventing us from not losing our shirt on it.

We couldn't move the car. We would have taken a killing by trading it in. We couldn't move it on the open market.

Well, two days after the layoff, I went down and had it refinanced which just killed me, but there was no other way to do it. It's not a comfortable way to do it. I've totaled another thousand dollars of paying interest. You know, it just irks you to do it.

I think I was dealing with it realistically. I was checking the figures, I was reading the papers, I was checking with my committeeman, I was looking for options. I was begging him to let me put the house on the market, and then putting it on the market.

A year ago. And yet, some people won't face it. It was like I've seen things go bad before. I said, You haven't seen already announced in the paper that three thousand are going to lose their jobs. And now the union tells me it's fifty-five hundred that have lost jobs.

Well, with the majority of the layoffs concentrated in three states, it's going to be around 17,500. We've already got over 11,500 in Flint alone, laid off from GM.

I don't know if you've received this reaction from others, but you probably have.

The job losses are just water over the damn and our president at the union hall will be the first one to tell you that. But three and a half years ago, when they negotiated through paragraph 96 in the national agreement (allowing people to be brought over from Fisher into Buick), it hurt us immensely. And there is no way you're going to get around it.

And we're not given the benefits as though we were sent out, and lost our job from a factory that was shut down. They just laugh and say, We don't give them the benefits. They didn't lose their job because of a factory closing.

Well, we certainly did. The people from Fisher came over, took our lower seniority jobs out of Buick. We're pushed out on the street and we would have been dealt with differently as though we had lost our jobs because of a plant closing, but we don't receive anything that we may have received under those arrangements.

See what I mean? It was a domino effect is the best way I can try to explain it to people.

Under paragraph 96, national agreement, those people supposedly click-click, follow their jobs. They didn't. They chose to flow anywhere they wanted to with their seniority, once they got to Buick.

But the way it benefitted GM and, naturally, really hurt the people, is that they were then not given benefits that may have been negotiated for someone who lost their job through a plant closing.

Thirty-eight hundred people head out the door at Buick over the last three and a half years because of a plant closing, basically. But they don't get benefits like that.

We're getting a reduced SUB-pay. And don't quote me on that, I know it's twenty percent but I believe there's already a ten percent [taken out] before the twenty percent. There's a reduction on SUB.

In my case and many others, but the time they've laid you off several times during the year, you went out with less than twenty-six unemployment weeks to begin with.

The other thing, speaking as a grandma and laughing at my situation (sighs), is the fact that I would hate to be like the man in the *Suburban News.*

The newspaper mentions a man with his five children, much younger than mine, losing a job with better than ten years. And you're just going, Ohhh.

A few years ago, I was on the border. I was ready to be forced out the door at Buick with over six hundred young men and women, mostly young men, with young families out of Final

Assembly. They were forced to go to Pontiac, to go to Detroit, to go to Lake Orion. They're not treated like the people at Fisher. And I don't have anything against them.

But the man across the street. I'm sitting here looking at his house now.

Back then, I had six years in at Buick, he had sixteen at Fisher. We knew it was happening. He was working with the union and so was I. We knew it was going to come down the tubes. Well before it happened.

He was the best man at my daughter's wedding.

It was going to be him or me. He's now working at Buick and I'm not and I'm not treated as though I lost my job because of a plant closing, either.

It's interesting. The training that's going to be held for us that they're negotiating still with the U. of M.-Flint (sighs) to give us a crash course for twelve weeks, some of these courses will pull up to fifteen college credits.

They're going to be paying, I believe the man from U. of M. said $280 a class. Sounds horribly high to me. So check that figure out.

In other words, U. of M.-Flint is charging General Motors and our tuition fund, each individual person's tuition fund, a full shot of money. I got the list on the classes and they're going to be having us on four different days of the week. Actually a total of six different days of the week in two different places, running to U. of M. for practice on the computers and running to Grand Blanc. Offering it on Tuesdays, Thursdays, and Fridays one month; Mondays and Wednesdays on another month; Saturday at another time and I thought, We're letting them suck up our tuition credits for this?

It's got to be because it's a crash course and they're doing the best they can to get the instructors. But it was crazy the way it was set up.

It's $5,500, the union told us, in tuition credits that we'll be given.

You can see what I mean. It's just a little aggravating when you're going: Wow. This is my precious tuition fund—all that I got out of this thing to start my life over with.

I'm trying to get the U. of M.-Flint classes straightened out— try and see if I might get some benefit from them. Checking into other avenues of training. I'd even gone as far as Georgia and Florida. Checked out the jobs. Found out what I'd make as a job setter in Florida. Found out what the best jobs that I could pull off in Atlanta would be. I could make $29 as an RN.

Florida because of the weather. After the operations on my

hands when they were tore up at Buick and the weather in Michigan didn't make them feel any better, so I thought, well, go south young woman. (Laughs.)

It was an option. General Motors was holding my family in this town. They aren't now. And I'm not going to sit here for years and wonder if they're going to tie me up again or not.

Well, it just happens to be that my husband's pay is very low in this town right now because his job's been affected [by the plants shutting down]. Ironically, he can transfer just about anyplace in the nation. So it did leave me with options.

Where would they pay me more for my hands after the operation at Buick? (Laughs)

I was advised just last week to check into disability benefits.

You wouldn't believe what I've tried . . . I put like, a resume in my head, as though I was doing a job resume. I went over it in my head, I wrote it down. This is what you've done, you know, from high school right on through.

Where are my strengths? Where are my weaknesses?

Where have I succeeded before? What skills do I have? A job setter is similar to what I have done. I'd be fighting, frankly, prejudice against hiring into a nonunion shop as a woman, a little bit older.

The base pay would be about $7.50 in Florida. It's not $3.35 an hour and that's what I'm facing in this town.

You want something interesting? Guess what I did yesterday.

I drove through swirling snow, down an expressway to Rochester, Michigan, following a son that was married very young, who needs a good job. And a son-in-law that has come back out here from Europe after being in the service and has also found himself in the position of needing a good job.

Followed these two young men who got hired into a small plastics company in Rochester. They couldn't find better work here in Flint without a college education.

They have hired in a plastics company called Superior Plastics starting out at $4.05 an hour. They are working on the same, if not the exact same machines, then certainly the same type of machines, that I ran at a little better than $9.00 an hour about six years ago in Plant 12 Plastics in the Buick complex. Making the same damn parts, excuse my French.

It's outsourcing that, thank goodness, didn't go over the border [to Mexico]. But my son is making one-fourth of what I made, compared to my wages when I left five weeks ago. He's making one-fourth of what I made.

They're automotive parts. They're going in our GM cars.

Well, of course they are. The kids know exactly where they're shipped.

They're hired in at $4.05 an hour; after ninety days, they'll have Blue Cross or comparable—some coverage, anyway—and will be given a 25 cent an hour raise. After ninety days, they'll make $4.30 an hour with some medical coverage.

And that is the same fan shroud, lease spring, kick plate, and plastic dash that I was working on—the same job I did before we lost the contract to do these jobs in what they call Plant 12 Plastics in the Buick complex.

And I was taking my daughter down there hoping she could hire in.

When I was on the picket line outside Final Assembly— before it was Buick City—about four years ago, we struck for a short period of time and I was there with my camper all night, the first night of the strike.

And the next morning I was interviewed by a man from CBS. And my backside ended up on the front page of the *Flint Journal.* That was cute! If you can picture me bending over, making signs for the union, frantically writing "Local 599" on our picket signs and passing them out to the guys and I'm bent over next to my own truck and camper, right? With nothing but size 14 backside showing and that hits the front of the *Journal.* It was great. But anyway.

The guy from CBS interviewed me, so it wasn't gossip. It was firsthand. He had come back from Mexico, the General Motors building that was going up down there.

And I was trying to brag about our complex, how big it is, three miles long, and how many we employ and I was excited about it. Before I even knew who he was or knew he was there to do an interview.

And he kept telling me who he was and that he had left Mexico and he said, "You should see what they're [GM] building in Mexico!" And he said, "They wouldn't let us in the factory gate. They wouldn't let us in the door. We had to interview an employee in his home which was a cinderblock that he was proud to have with his 66 cent an hour wages at GM." And this man was just appalled and aggravated that GM wouldn't let . . . oh, they didn't want that kind of PR.

And I could see what was happening then and now to my sons, this one that I'm following down and seeing him work at a job that's going to be $4.30 after ninety days on the job doing the same thing I did.

Yeah, it scares me. It certainly does. And it makes me feel that there's something above and beyond just General Motors involved in it because it's our protectionism we don't have through our government. It's the outsourcing on GM's part.

You read your stockholders' report. And it's all written so differently. It's not what you see in the newspapers. It's presented very differently to stockholders. It's like now I have $56 worth of stock for a year and no job. That's not the way Roger Smith wrote it up in the stockholders' report.

You ought to read that thing. That's something else. They're making money this year despite "slight inconveniences." Hah! I'm one of the slight inconveniences!

Now, I'm not focusing in as much on the anger I'm feeling, but on the way I felt going to Rochester. With one-third of my family going down there to work for wages at $4.05 starting pay, doing what I used to do for $12. That got me. And going eighty miles a day to do it.

I told my kids, we've been drop-kicked, knocked right out of the middle class. And you're seeing it happen right now. And that's anger and I'm sorry, but I feel it.

It's the first generation, they say, that is not going to be able to really feel that they're going to do better than their parents.

I did better than my folks, thank goodness, thanks to GM and my husband did better earlier on his job. Before, like I said, his back and kids in the hospital and things hit us. Even as a life insurance salesman. He still did well, better, without a college education with courses and passing state boards and stuff that he did for that job.

His father was an electrician at GM. His mother sold china part-time on the side and raised four kids.

But we still did well. Though we can't guarantee that for our children.

It's seeing that happen to them that really hurts. I mean you can't get more reality than seeing the machinery they're working on. And knowing the wages in a nonunion shop that they're drawing.

My father was a union steward and maybe I'm too prounion. But I can see the difference.

Some of us, the women, were talking just before we lost our jobs. Maxine went out of there the same day I did.

Maxine is about thirty-six; she's newly married. Had worked as a security guard in stores before she hired in at Buick.

We're checking into a job as a security guard. They're not hiring in the Genesee County jails, but we've already checked into jails and talked to guards—women guards—to find where the other jobs are available. 'Cause they're over $9 an hour.

These women go in at $9 an hour and they don't have any training. Believe me, I'd get my own. Because the experience they had in August, you know the killing of that guard?

She's checking into it because it's similar to what she had done before. She also runs her own business on the side. But I'm not getting back with her because I talked to a corrections officer in the Genesee County Jail and she told me the ones in Ionia might be some of the better ones to work in.

But anyway, we checked into that. I signed up for the computer classes. I've done sales you know, worked in sales part-time. What I've actually signed up for is the classes through U. of M.-Flint. I sat there all day Monday at the union hall to get information.

What was so discouraging about those training courses, was that I found out there were only twenty-five available spots per listed occupation, three, and they've got hundreds of us sitting there.

I've got June 18 looking me in the eye. That's when the money runs out.

People on the street would ask me, Well, you're married aren't you? Well, hubby will take care of you. Well, you have your husband to rely on, don't you? Well, what the hell, you're only taking a man's job anyway. Well, what have you got to worry about? Your kids are almost raised. Well, so do something about your bills. I'm telling you what people have said to me.

Another one: Oh, well you've got a couple of years of income at full hundred percent coming in don't you? Oh, your unemployment lasts a year, doesn't it? Oh, you make pretty good unemployment, don't you? Those are some of the things I've heard.

You'd think this town, with as many people that work at GM, would be more educated about the real situation. And they're not.

People really don't give a damn. (Laughs.) I was surprised. I was surprised that my own, oldest daughter who lives in Millington was really, really not understanding. The general consensus was, You should live like a king if you work at GM.

Also, the assumption is, many, many times, if I work in the shop, my husband does. They don't know he made $600 last month. The assumption is, Well, you both work in the shop, don't you?

It's unbelievable.

This town has been up and down before and they just didn't believe this was going to happen permanently. This town has said,

Oh, we had a bad year in '72. Oh, it was bad in the early fifties. Oh, don't worry about it. They didn't believe it was going to happen.

When I left the SUB office today and headed over to Region One and left there and the Training Center, and then I cut through the back side of a clothing store to get something to eat and I talked to the owner.

She said, "I hope this town turns around." They've had Terry Allen Plumbing and Heating, her and her husband for twenty-two years. She owns a clothing shop across the street on Fenton Road. She's got clothes hanging on the rack. Two-piece outfits for a $106. Yeah, you better believe she hopes it turns around.

And she is intelligent in that she was trying to get educated. She was asking me, "Well, how is it? How much is your money reduced by when you're drawing SUB? How does it look? Do you really think that AC will do something when they buy out Chevy? Do you think they'll do anything with the Fisher Plant? What have you heard about?"

She's trying. At least she's trying. She knows her business. Her husband has been in Terry Allen Plumbing and Heating for twenty-two years and her business, a clothing/apparel shop, depends on this town.

Yeah, people are trying to understand the situation and they're scared if they're running their own business.

I was so upset with my husband for not understanding my pain, not understanding my agony. After over ten years not knowing where the heck that budget's going. All he knows is that he covers the house payment and his haircut and the car insurance. And the life insurance is drawn out of his paycheck, you know.

He hadn't paid anything else in so many years, he couldn't fathom the hurt we were going to be feeling. Finally he fathomed it when I forced him to make a united budget.

Another thing, again, it's from a woman's viewpoint. And I talked to several women and they kept expressing it just before I left there. They had done a nontraditional job. They had done what was traditionally men's work.

They had found their language not exactly pristine like when they had started at Buick. (Laughs.)

One of them said, "Knowing my mouth, I would probably be comfortable in a similar situation. Not in an office working just with women. I've become comfortable in working with men and the way they view an objective that has to be accomplished. Men are goal-oriented. Get with it and do it."

A lot of these women were expressing that viewpoint.

I've been changed by the experience of working in the shop. I'm different. I'm not the way I was nine, ten, eleven, twelve years ago.

Denise was telling me that. Maxine was telling me that. They said, I'm not that comfortable working with women in a traditional woman's job.

The experience has changed me.

It's like when something that's ninety pounds has to be picked up, I go over and I pick it up. I move it. I see a man start to move something and I say, Whoa, let me help you.

I don't think about it twice.

I was with a group of boy scouts and the men were all in the boats. I stepped away from the women and their pretty picture hats and I grabbed hold of the boat and heaved. It changes you. You learn to pitch in. You learn to work with the men. You learn to not be that little lady in the white gloves.

And you say how has it changed me? And am I going to fit back in?

Your expectations are raised because you've also become a little more aggressive. You've also become a little more individualized—a little stronger. A little more self-reliant. You've done things you've never thought you could have done. You've looked in the guts of a machine that would have scared the royal tar out of you and you've said, I'll change that sucker. I'll grab that part. I'll grab those cutters. I'll pull them off there. It's not going to scare me. I'll do it. I can handle it.

You go to break loose a bolt and you can't get it 'cause you're not strong enough to budge the thing. You know your job relies on it and you go down to the tool machine shop and you get a welder and you get some pipe and you say, Hey, make me a cheater bar on this sucker. And you have a foot and a half cheater bar put on the end of your wrench and you break that bolt loose and you do that job.

And there's no way but to say it's changed you.

Like good ol' Rosie the Riveter, right? I don't know if it started the women's movement but I think the only other experience that is similar is a farmer's wife. She's out there, doing what he's doing. You know, that's another example.

Just to go in and sell clothing off the rack and worry about how my nail polish looks and to listen to the chitchat and the backstabbing and working solely with women . . . I don't know . . . I don't know. And I'm not the only woman who feels this way.

I feel a responsibility to my children not only in do I feel cheated? Do I feel let down about the expectations I've got as a woman, to go out there and to go to work again? Not only as a GM employee, the guys have got to feel the same way. Where am I going to pull down the same wages?

And doubly for a woman. Where am I going to pull down the same wages? I've gotten used to them.

I know how to rough it. I've raised five kids with a husband on seventy-two bucks a week. I know how to rough it. Do I want to go back to that?

And I know the men, the men feel that way. But I do think it's doubly hard for some of the women. I really do. And you really want to worry about whether you break a nail?

Things take on a different—and I'm giving the guys credit. I mean, a lot of the work ethics that you learn, working with the guys. If you go in there and you say, (uses a southern belle accent) "Oh, mah goodness, that fan'll mess up mah hair. Well, honey, can you lift this? Well, I can't do that." Well, then you're not going to change and you're not really going to be pulling your weight.

But, hey, if I'm making the same wages they are, I'll do the job. You may end up with your hands tore up like I did, but you sure gave it your best shot.

I mean, I give the guys credit.

You take a little old lady like me out there for fifteen years and not doing it and then jumping in with both feet, you know. I did come out changed by the experience, I really did.

And my husband had a lot of changing to do with me because it was like, Whoa, what have I got on my hands, here? I want from Suzy Homemaker to . . . twenty-six years of marriage and what have I got now? You know? (Laughs.)

If God wanted me to cook, why didn't he make a restaurant sign out front, you know? (Laughs.)

Well, Denise was making the joke, "Oh, my goodness, my mouth!" She said, "I can just see, with my mouth, the trouble I'd get into in a job working with just women." She said, "I have been . . ."—I used the word roughened—but she said, "I have developed a mouth on me." She's been in about twelve years. And she said, "I didn't really want to, it just seemed to happen."

And jokingly saying how she was comfortable in the nontraditional women's jobs that she's done and working with machinery.

Like we didn't need a foreman in our area. We worked as a team. That part from coal-header through shavers. Machining operations through the arvids, through the hobs, through shavers, through the Olsons, from when it started right at coal-headers, right on through.

We worked as a team. I was the only woman. I was the only

job setter, but I kept forgetting I was a woman. I kept forgetting that fact. So, if I wanted to know how they were doing over in Olsons and how our slowest stock was, or if I wanted to know how we were doing over in arvids, I tried not to make a pest of myself, but I'd check with the guys. And they, in turn, would check with me. Well, how we doing?

How's our quality on the computer? Go in, pull it up, check each machining department and see where we're at, see where our fullest stock was, see how we were doing. Work together as a team.

You have to work together because when you're working with a machine you're working with what people can mess up or what that machine can mess up. And if you know that the Olson doesn't put out a straight cut, it's going to affect the taper of your gears when you cut the tooth. It's going to affect the taper. Your chancellor can be wrong on the cut of the tooth.

You know that if you're having a problem and it's hanging up on your arbor, it's maybe three machining operations down the line that's caused that. So you get back with the outfit operator. Because your foreman's never around. And you get in there and look.

And you say, I think we've got a problem here and it's going from arvid to Olson and when it hits my hobs then my arbor has to clamp down tighter under greater pressure and it's a tighter fit. And now I'm seeing that we're cutting this, the i.d.s too small.

You work together as a team or you don't put out a good product. And we had a damn good product going out.

Women, their feelings have been so strong. You'd think the men's were strong because it's such a heavy-duty thing to be the breadwinner, but damn it, I'm the breadwinner here, too. And so my feelings are the same as the men and compounded worse.

They're getting on with it. They know the responsibilities there. They have to move.

When I sat down and I analyzed strengths and weaknesses and past experiences and job experiences and what people have told me, they said, "You got a mouth on you. You can make your point. You can draw people to you." And I've had some work in sales and helping my husband with his line of business. I was also manager for twelve people in sales part-time before I started in at Buick.

But . . . my wildest daydream when I got all done, you put it all together, it looks like the best thing I could do is manage heavy-duty machinery. (Laughs.)

I'm hoping something will come out of those classes [at UM-

Flint]. But I don't want to be putting my life on hold in hopes that I get the class.

If they called me back this soon, I would go. But I'm not going to put my life on hold for them.

I'm walking down the line, I've seen my children's lives barely being eked out with families to raise because they've married young. And my son is a senior assistant now he's going to be managing his own shop in Lansing at Action Auto. He's moved up about two years faster than normally. He's only going to be twenty-one.

And his wife is the youngest manager in the shoe department at Value City in Lansing. They both transferred from Flint. They were married just a few weeks ago. November 7. My other son has had some electronics training and left Channel 25 and he's the one going down to Rochester at $4.30 an hour after he gets his ninety days in. And that, that scares me.

My best advice to other people is that you may bottom out. And then, once you hit bottom, you've gotta bounce up 'cause there's no place else left to go.

And don't be surprised if you feel, like they said at the union hall, men or women find themselves being uptight. Just ornery. Ornery with their spouses. Ornery with their kids. Get the heck down there and talk to somebody. Work it out. And admit that your feelings may hit bottom for a while and then you bounce back.

You're going to have to face it. And you might hit bottom. You're going to have to have your partner face it. Analyze your strengths and weaknesses and past experiences in work, what you've done and your own personality. And check in.

Be knowledgeable. If it takes a consultant, a lawyer, your union, get out there—get the information. Go for it. Learn. Find out who can help you and how. Find out what's available.

A year ago, I was checking on job opportunities for my husband and I both, whether it was out of state. Asking which one of the kids might be willing to move. Since then we've had two new marriages, too, so it also involves their spouses.

Not as much as I could have, still, in taking my own advice. That's what I was doing this week is getting information again.

Even to the point of forcing myself to type and type and type to find out how it affects my hands. Because grabbing a heavy-duty wrench and changing some tooling on a machine doesn't tell you what your small motor coordination is, exactly. I know I can't sew in the morning. Don't ask me to sew on a button in the morning because my hands hurt and they don't work.

I'm wondering, can I be fast enough on a computer to do it? You know. Again, it was strengths and weaknesses. How badly have my hands been affected?

Now, you asked me how I feel about being laid off. Well.

I think it was August 3. (Sighs). I headed into work on second shift. Now, for some reason, I didn't take the expressway that day. I had to veer off to pay a bill or something.

And I ended up driving down Dort Highway and I looked up ahead of me. And there was a mass of air-filled balloons like great, big party balloons in multicolors. Sticking up in what appeared to be the middle of Dort Highway. What they turned out to be was an advertisement for a tuxedo shop.

But all you could see, looking down Dort Highway ahead of you was this massive display of balloons, all in bright colors, hanging up there in the sky like somebody's holding them up for a party.

And beyond them, masses, masses of black smoke just rolling up from the vicinity of Buick. And it was the weirdest thing. I sketched a little drawing when I got into work. And I said, My town. Our town. Buick and GM. Like the party's over.

The way it hit me, I knew my job was over and four days later I was laid off.

Hatch/Benton

In March and April of 1987, I wrote two feature stories that appeared in the Flint Journal as part of the Life After the Line series. Each involved an entrepreneur: Craig Hatch, twenty-nine and Lawrence M. Benton, thirty-six. These young men had worked on the line at General Motors for ten years and had slowly built up separate businesses while working.

Benton elected to take a voluntary layoff to pursue his wood-cutting business full-time: he cut trees and sold firewood and tinder. Hatch inherited a gravel and black dirt hauling business from his grandfather which he built into Hatch Enterprise, a parking lot and lawn maintenance service.

Each had a considerable investment in their businesses.

Hatch had more than $77,000 invested in equipment alone. He was able to employ up to eighteen seasonal full-time employees, and he often wore a beeper during his second shift job as line repairman at the Flint Assembly Plant of General Motors Truck and Bus Group.

Benton estimated he was in debt about $70,000. Besides buying the land, sixty-one wooded acres in Montrose Township, he invested in machinery, including three trucks, a logskidder, chain saws, a conveyer belt, and a hydraulic logsplitter. He employed only himself and his wife, figuring to make at least $45,000 profit after the first year.

Taken together, both stories resonate with the individual's determination and desire to grow and change. Both men are risk-takers in uncertain times.

How much risk? Interviewed almost a year later, each had significant changes to report.

When Hatch's story ran on March 1, 1987, he was still

working full-time while operating Hatch Enterprise. He had told me, "I'd just as soon they'd shut down. It would give me more time for my business." Part of that quote appeared in the newspaper headline.

According to Hatch, his fellow workers' reactions were harsh.

They just really ragged on me. Not my close friends, but people who didn't know me that well. They thought I should just get out if I was so anxious for a shutdown. And so I did. They were really angry.

What's the point of staying there, I thought. The business is still successful. So now I'm out.

I got a lot of flack on that story. Mostly because of the headline. People just didn't read the whole story. But I'm prepared.

You can't depend on the shop, anyway. When I first hired in, the business wasn't very big, but I could see the shop wasn't the place for a real career. I was laid off three times before. And now I'm glad I'm out.

In fact, I was in a parade in Swartz Creek with my machinery, in a float down the main street. And I even heard somebody call out something smart because of that story.

But, you know, I've gotten a lot of contracts from people who read it, too, a lot of business contacts. I guess they thought I was serious enough about my business. They wanted to hire me to do a good job.

And at my son's school, the principal even called me about the story and said he thought I did a good thing. You know, so many people just wait and there I was getting something accomplished on my own. And I like being my own boss.

I mean, it's work, but it's good.

So, I guess it's been both bad and good. I was planning on getting out of there, anyway. So, it just happened a little sooner than I thought.

I think the people facing layoffs need to get out and find something else to do. They need more drive, instead of waiting around.

One person who didn't wait around was Larry Benton. But his risk was in no way as successful as Hatch's, although it seemed more lovely as he spoke about the positive change in family lifestyle at the time.

He, his wife Debbie Reid Benton, and their three sons, aged from eight to ten years old, all enjoyed being in the woods as part of the firewood selling business.

Debbie just loves the woods. She can outwork any man I could hire. And the kids fish in a little pond and then they haul and help on deliveries.

You can work without someone standing over your shoulder all the time.

I just got tired of the rumors of layoffs, the constant yo-yo and seesaw. I decided to take a chance.

When I was a kid, I worked summers on my grandmother's tobacco farm in the south, so I'm used to farm hours. A friend suggested that we cut and sell firewood for extra money for Christmas and I started really getting into it.

We had the cutting rights for this land, and I eventually bought out the other guy. Then I finally bought the land outright.

It's long hours—ten to twelve hours a day—but it's harder for me to stand in that little square on the line for eight hours than to move in the woods all day.

There's just so much more self-satisfaction with wood-cutting.

You can see what you've accomplished at the end of each day. It's not just another steel body going down the line.

You have plenty of nervous stomach days, maintaining the equipment. In the beginning, I was more upset. But you learn.

I learned that if you have the right tools, you can fix anything.

When I first started, I didn't know one tree from another. Now I know all of them. We cut hardwood, red oak and white, hard maple, some ash, cherrywood, sassafras, and birch for the holidays.

We cut conservatively, and leave the younger trees, trees less than eight inches wide.

The way they're talking, when my kids grow up there won't be a lot of jobs, either. And by that time, eight or nine years, those same trees will be ready to cut.

The only security is in yourself.

DEBBIE: I never thought I'd be a lumberjack. But this is the best thing that's ever happened to us. It's so beautiful in the woods when the machinery stops and you can hear the birds.

It's a different story a year later. The Benton's are divorced. They lost their home. The original business has been dissolved, although Benton has begun a second attempt at the same business.

Debbie and Larry have been unavailable for comment.

107

9
Rhodes

Listening to Dave Rhodes is like hearing your favorite uncle tell a story. Part of his job is to make people feel comfortable when they sit across from him and he's good at it.

This tall, thin man with graying hair, light blue eyes, and an easy handshake, has been hired by the UAW–GM Human Resource Center as a job developer. This is who you see for the economic thread that stitches your family back together. He works behind the scenes, makes the connections, talks to businesses, sets up interviews, gives you your chance. He is viewed as the godfather of the Human Resource team in the eyes of laid-off workers.

Just before our 1:00 appointment, Rhodes took a few minutes to talk with Remon Daniel, a laid-off worker whom he had just placed in a new career as an auto mechanic. The job paid about $7 an hour and included educational and health benefits. Having been on an extended layoff twice before himself, he has a special understanding of what the clients, as they are called, experience.

Although Rhodes is part of the joint effort by General Motors and the United Auto Workers he had not previously worked for either. His background is in business, which helps in his efforts to contact potential employers.

The UAW–GM Human Resource Center—or the HRC as it is commonly called by laid-off workers—has funds to supplement the pay workers receive at their new jobs to help workers make the transition from high-paying auto jobs to lower paying ones outside of the auto industry. For instance, if a new job pays only $5 an hour, HRC will supplement that pay up to $5.00 for a certain time. So the worker receives as much as $10 an hour for a selected time period.

*His hard-to-refuse offer is hope for a new life and he hands it
out through on-the-job training programs, job clubs, supplemental job contracts, and developing workers' skills for jobs that will
be available in the future. But he is the godfather all the same;
you feel as if he has all of the answers.*

Like many other people, I was unemployed. I started out
with the Chamber of Commerce in Flint. Did job development
with them. I was hired as a developer. It was a new experience
for me.

They've done different surveys. I worked on a survey last
summer with the Chamber before I came here, contacting employers, discussing job requirements. It was used by this center to help
determine the scope of these training programs, to help determine
the curriculum.

In other words, we went right to the horse's mouth. We said,
"If you have a person in this job category, what do they do? What
do they have to know?" And that was used somewhat to gear the
curriculum for the center.

Several years ago, the Chamber of Commerce had a short-
term contract with this Human Resource Center to assist dislo-
cated autoworkers to find employment. That was my first experience.

So I had worked with autoworkers before. The people that
operate this center were familiar with my results and I think
that's why I was hired.

I think originally, the Chamber was trying to get a cross
section of people. And I came from a business background. So I
think I understand some of the problems that business has.

I can think a little bit as an employer. Too many people tend
to think about their own world and they don't stop to think about
what's going through the other party's mind. And I try and tell
people: Think as an employer. What is this employer looking for?

This employer doesn't care whether you have five kids or
one kid. It may be important to you, but it's not important to the
employer. The employer is interested in one thing: Do you have
something that will make this a better organization? When I get
done paying you is there going to be something left over?

I was hired at HRC because I have a good reputation as a job
developer. There are two stages to job development.

One, you have to identify the jobs. But just identifying the
jobs does not take care of the problem. Then you get into a match-
ing process. Is this the right employee for the employer? You
know, skill level, attitude, etc. Maybe driving distance is a factor.

Is this the right job for our client? In other words, if a person has skills that require $8.00 an hour, obviously, they're not going to survive on a job that pays $5.00. On the other hand, we may have a problem that their skill might not justify $8.00 an hour outside of GM.

Their needs might be there, but when you get away from GM there's a real strong tie-in between a person's skill or educational level and the pay. And that is hard.

Through the center we have a lot of structured training programs. I have been really active in setting up on-the-job training programs. We not only try to get a person a skill, but we also do leverage wages a little bit.

We won't write one [a supplemental pay job contract] for less than $5.50. To date, I have not written one that's less than $6 and I've written some as high as $10.

I approach it from the psychological aspect, you know, we want to make this thing work. And to work, the person has to have the opportunity to get a good skill.

They have to, obviously, have the requirements necessary to enter the trade. Maybe they have a low skill, but again, an attitude is part of it. They have to, I think, have a real interest. Not everybody should become an electrician, not everybody should become a pipe fitter or an accountant.

We are all individuals. So I'm saying that I hate to place somebody in a job simply because they need a job. Now, that may be a fact of life, they have to have a job. But I don't want to place somebody, especially in a good job, and have them say later, This is not for me.

Then you've blown their credibility. The employer's upset. And this is a problem, especially as people run out of benefits. They say, Hey, get me something, help me get something.

Well, I think we have to face that a lot of people, I feel, weren't in love with their jobs at GM. They were in love with the money. To me, that is reality.

I am finding pretty much a general attitude saying, *I had it good. It was great while it lasted. But it's not there now. Were do we go next!*

Like: *I know I'm not going to make as much money as GM, but I'd like to make a living wage and see some opportunity.* This is a prevalent attitude.

Another prevalent thing is frustration, whether a person expresses it or not. I'd say probably everybody I deal with is frustrated. A few of them are angry. Fortunately for me, I think the counselors here get this more up front when they enter the system.

See, typically, they're in the system a little while before I enter into a relationship with them.

People hear the words "job developer" and they look at me as the life raft that they can climb onto. And really, this is not the case. I do a lot of employment counseling, although I'm not hired as a counselor. I do it because I simply have to do something with these people. I hate to turn a person away. I feel these people are hurting.

I think we're being unfair to say, "Oh, gee, I'm a job developer. I'll get you a job, don't worry about anything." Doesn't work that way.

See, in a job developer, you need a mix. You need to spend time with the employers and you need to be familiar with your clients. But I have so many people wanting to see me that I am not doing my job right in contacting employers.

And I think it's interesting, the concept here. That this is a team between GM and the UAW which almost becomes a new entity in itself. And it's hard to say who I really work for. I don't work for the UAW and I don't work for GM. I am working as an independent contractor but I guess I'm working for a joint venture.

As I see it, all decisions are made jointly. You know, one or the other doesn't make a decision without touching base and deciding together. And I think that's very interesting.

I think, too, that maybe it's symbolic of the future, that somehow, there really has to be cooperation between unions and management. With staff.

And I was going to say that I have found a change in employer attitude. I don't really feel that I'm running into extreme anger against former GM employees like there was a couple of years ago. There's some. But I think the big fear they had a couple of years ago was that if I hire this person, they're going to get called back. And because of the economic climate changing so much, that fear has been dissipated somewhat.

And again, some employers have this stereotype. They hear these stories about the guy on third shift sleeping up in the rafters. They don't hear about the good people.

I counteract that. I say, Do you have any neighbors that work for GM? They say, Yeah. I say, Are they nice people? They say, Yeah. I say, Are they honest? They say, Yeah. I say, How about relatives, do you have any relatives that work for GM? And pretty soon, I swing over and I say, Now, wait a minute. You know, you talked about GM workers and I'm sure there are some GM workers that are not worth their salt. But for every bad one, there's a thousand good ones. So let's look at people as individuals.

Or they might say, I had a GM worker here ten years ago and I had a bad experience. Indicating that they're afraid of having another bad experience. I guess one thing that I see that they need is good PR on the part of employees. A lot of employers are not aware of what we have. Now, we've had a little bit [good PR] and partly it's that our workload is so heavy that it's been hard to develop a strategy and work it with available personnel to let employers know who we are, what we can offer, and what we've got available.

This really is a good service for employers who take advantage of it. If, as a job developer, I do my job right, the employers have got a good thing going.

Now, recently, they have added some temporary help. Two people. Very capable people. And I am training them to go out and do some of the things I do. The only problem is that my case load is so high—so many people want to see me that I'm having trouble training the new people.

But I am working on the assumption that these are very intelligent people. I'm telling them go out there and do it. You're better off doing it and making mistakes than to have me do nothing. When you have mistakes, when you have problems, then we'll talk about it.

That's the way I learned this business. Except I had nobody there to bail me out. At least the ones I'm training have somebody to bail them out if they run into something.

Now, the autoworkers . . . I think here there is a psychological aspect. Many of these people, their father worked for GM, their grandfather worked for GM, you know, some of them are third generation autoworkers. They have become accustomed in a, let's say, a firm routine. And, a little bit like the army, they really didn't have to worry; you know, they made enough money to keep a roof over their heads, they had good medical coverage and all these things.

And I think GM was like a security blanket.

Now, I'm not criticizing these people, I'm just saying it's sort of a pattern that you fall into. In other words, every day you can get up and know that today is going to be like yesterday. Okay. And to some people that is reassuring.

But not only at GM, I think worldwide, you've reached a point where you don't know what's going to happen today.

I have had people come in here and say, "All I want is a decent job that has security." And I say, "I'm sorry but you have come to the wrong place." My own job, I have two weeks security.

I can terminate or the people who pay me can terminate and it's right in a contract.

So I have two week security. And I'd say a lot of people don't realize, for example, that any time you take a job, whether it's spoken or unspoken, there is a trial period. A point at which you're observed and they're trying to figure out, Did I pick the right person?

Now, the employer might spell that out and say, Hey, you're on a thirty day trial period, but many, many times it is unspoken and people have to live with this.

So of course, they have these five or ten years security where they didn't have to worry about re-establishing themselves, their reputation with a new employer. It's a tough adjustment, really.

People need a base of skills. Absolutely. I'd say a high skilled person will probably not be out of work too long.

The problem, as I see it, let's say at this point in history, the nation is riding fairly low unemployment. In fact, unemployment is decreasing. The state of Michigan, in spite of all the layoffs, has more jobs now than they had a year ago. More people working.

The sad part is that many of them are in the service industry and the pay is not adequate for one person to support a family.

The other factor is that we've become entrenched, you know, as you buy your home. You raise a family. You may get involved with a church, social activities, and what have you. Friends, neighborhoods.

And if you have to decide, Am I going to stay or leave? It's a tough, tough decision.

Most people at this point are saying, If I have to, I will move. I really don't want to. In my opinion, about two percent of the people at this point in time are relocation minded.

As people run out of benefits, I predict that a lot of people are going to move. Not because they want to, but because there's nothing else for them.

I think our latest unemployment figure is somewhere around fifteen percent in Genesee County. And regardless of what you hear, there are a lot of people that don't get counted. They fall through the cracks. They're not registered for employment services through MESC, they are not collecting benefits.

I don't know how they arrive at these figures, but I suspect that the typical figure is about five percent low. If they tell you fifteen you've probably got twenty.

Certain parts of the country, they have an opposite problem. They cannot get enough people. The unemployment rate in

Connecticut is three percent. In Massachusetts it's 2.7 percent. And I've talked to the MESC office on the other side of the state. They tell me they have a problem in reverse.

We have people and not enough jobs and they have jobs and don't have enough people.

If people were like checkers and we could move them around anyplace we wanted, the majority of people could have jobs.

When somebody advertises for a journeyman electrician in the Flint paper for a job in Grand Rapids it's because they don't have very many electricians in Grand Rapids. Otherwise, why advertise here?

Yeah, it's funny, most fast food places are minimum wage here. But when you get out of Genesee County, as close to us as Brighton, I have seen signs out where they would start people at fast food places at $4.25 an hour.

But, if you were an economics student of the law of supply and demand, our price is regulated to some degree not only by our values but by the marketplace.

We are, in other words, a commodity and that's a tough thing. . . . We're unique; no two people have the same fingerprints in the whole world, yet in the job market sometimes we are lumped into a situation where we are just one of the many.

Let me cover two things. Let me talk about our pool of people.

Other groups work with pools of people—you know, disadvantaged people, youth, older workers or what have you.

But I'm saying that our pool of people, when it comes down to work experience and skill, the autoworkers are the best in this whole area.

Several reasons. A lot of these people have taken advantage of training offered through GM. A lot of them have used their TAPP funds. I am running into people with four year degrees. Not just an occasional one, but a fair number. I'm running into people with associates degrees. I'm running into people who have had specialized training.

This is a good group of people. My opinion of the majority of them is that they are quality people. Like every group, there always is some bad apples. But I'm saying the majority. We not only have quality skills but we have quality people. And I mean that. I tell employers that.

It's true.

Somebody that's motivated, you know. Has good personal habits. You hear all the horror stories about drunks and, you know, dope, what have you, and I'm sure there's some of it in GM.

But I'm saying that of the people coming through here, they are high caliber people.

Now this is a volunteer program. I might say we don't necessarily have everybody that's eligible using the services. Of course, if you put out a book, we might get flooded!

Anytime we get publicity we get huge numbers of people calling.

Another thing I was going to bring out—if I had five clones we would still be ineffective. We sell this idea: we are your partner to help you find a job. We call it self-search.

We will help you. Self-directed job search. We are promoting self-directed job search. We have job clubs which are groups of maybe ten, twelve people who get together on a regular basis. They share their problems, they share leads. The go out and knock on doors and maybe they find some jobs that they can't get that might apply to somebody else in the job club, see. It's a support group.

I'd say that seventy-five percent of what happens in a job club is psychological. Number one: they got away from the house and they find out they're not alone in the world. They have a chance to talk with people who are in similar circumstances.

Now, I was in the first job club as the facilitator. Almost everybody that was in that club is now working except for a few dropouts.

People say: I don't know why, but I feel better when I leave here than when I come in. In other words, they're hurting, these people, see. And I think that helps get rid of some of that, the job club.

There's this club, too, called Over 40. It's a national network of nonprofit job clubs for people over forty years of age. We do not have a chapter here. Ours is Mickey Mouse compared to theirs. We have people for a couple hours a week. You come into the Over 40 club like you're going to a job, five days a week. You're told what your assignment is and you do it. And to get into it, you have to meet these requirements.

Our requirements are very, very lenient.

I'm sure a spouse gets awful tired of hearing: Well, I went out today and I didn't get a job. We're dealing with how it gets to be old. Here you get a chance to get away from that. Here, you share your misery a little bit.

Where do you see yourself in the next year or so?

I can only guess, you know. My contract is an annual contract that expires in August. I feel that if I want to continue, there's going to be at least another year. I see the need, you know. The need is going to be there.

We got a lot of people from Fisher. Now, you might want to check on this. Rather than have three thousand people walk in here, they're trying to do some off-site work because we are flooded right now.

I'd say this staff, they're dedicated. I think they're fortunate to have the staff they do. I'm not just talking about mysef, I'm just saying the counselors, the trainers, really professional people.

I'd say they don't have a staff member here that won't cut their lunch short, stay over if necessary to help a client, without pay.

I have mixed feelings, quite frankly. I'm a good job developer. And I think that to be a good job developer you have to care for people. But there's a tremendous amount of frustration. Before I took this job I said to myself, I will never be a job developer again.

It isn't that I don't like it. I like it. And it's rewarding. But I think it's a self-destructive career. Some people call it burnout. I don't think anybody can go on being an effective job developer year after year after year. In other words, you have to get away from it.

Number one, you're dealing with frustration on the part of everybody you talk to. Even if they have a high skill, they're down.

And secondly, in reality there's some people that your probability of helping . . . I won't say it's impossible, but in this job market, it's going to be tough. At least as far as putting them into what I would call a living wage.

There again, when I came in here, I felt the two problems I had to deal with the most, you know, the toughest ones—What do I do with a person with a four year degree in business administration?

Throughout the country management positions have been pared. Everybody's gotten lean and mean. And these are the people that went. So it means there's a lot of them out there. You know, with good skills but very little demand.

The other problem I had to deal with in my own way was . . . say, okay, here's this person that came off the line who twisted the same bolt eight hours a day. What can I do to help them get a living wage?

Because their skill level away from GM might only get them four or five dollars an hour. In reality. And here I see our on-the-job training programs as a solution for some of these people.

Like, we've got the two women who are becoming electricians. When they first went in there they were probably a little overwhelmed, but then they got more comfortable.

That's the purpose of a training program. In this case, the employer was not looking for high skills, the employer was looking for attitude and the ability to learn. Also, the employer believed that women do that type of work much better than men because they are neater.

And he may be right. You know, I'm not biased for or against women, but I'm just saying that he may be right that some jobs, somehow, women adapt to better than men.

Well, let's face it: Men are not women and women are not men. I have known of cases where women have accepted very physical jobs to get the big money but could not handle it. Now, that's not true of all women. I've known some women that, physically, were stronger than men. But I'm saying, generally speaking, I feel there are some jobs that are more suited for women and some jobs that are more suited for men.

Now, I guess the women's lib wouldn't like to hear me say that.

The interesting thing about Faith Ellis is that I have placed her twice now. I placed her roughly three years ago when she was laid off. And our paths crossed again. The big difference now is that she's in a job where she should be able to acquire a skill which will give her more security. The last time she was driving a truck.

She's a very nice person, very outgoing. Super personality.

I worked an on-the-job training contract in Florida just this morning. I have a person who's going on electrician's training in Florida, starting next Monday. We sell the concept that you find an employer who's willing to hire you and train you with our help. Let us know who it is. We will go out there and establish communication with the employer and see what we can work out to make it possible.

I'm trying to make them into their own job developers. Now, if I had to go out and find some employer who's willing to train somebody, I might have to talk to fifty employers. And if they find one, my productivity really increases. In other words, we're trying to help them become their own job developers. There's nothing wrong with that. I think we have to take that approach.

Now to employers, I try to sell the concept that I am not biased. I am the go-between. And I find this reassures employers to have this. I am not trying to take a bad person and get them a job. I have good people. I'm trying to establish their needs, the needs of the employer and try and come up with the right package deal where everybody's a winner.

I want them to last. I don't want to find somebody a job where they're going to quit. I would like it to last.

And it's funny, employers are not as fair in their capacity. Employers, a lot of them, expect unlimited loyalty from the people they hire, but they are not willing to dispense that loyalty themselves.

They'd like to hire you with the attitude you will stay with the employer forever. But the employer wants to be free to let you go tomorrow if things get tough.

The thing that amazes me as a job developer is not only the number of people laid off, but the length of service that they have and the skill level. And I feel bad in a way.

I feel that people are a natural resource the same as you might consider Lake Huron or Lake Michigan. They're something we're very fortunate to have. And if you don't believe me, check with the western states. They want to run a pipe, siphon out our water out west.

The same thing is happening in the job market to some extent. We are losing some of our best people. Our most skilled people because there is not enough work here. Not because they want to go.

The highest skilled people can typically afford to move because a skilled trades person will earn, not what they left at GM, but probably $12 an hour away from GM. Now, what they made at GM, I imagine they were making two, three, four dollars an hour more.

And I have done that. I have taken what I feel are the cream of the crop and exported them. So from a community standpoint, I think it is unfortunate that this is happening.

And my own feeling is—and I don't want to be quoted exactly—our answer is not in Genesee County job developers, although they have a useful purpose. Our real answer is economic development. We need to attract employers to this area. We have more people looking for work out there than there are jobs.

I guess, if I were laid off, I would do a lot of things, I'd tell you all if I had time.

I'd say, One: I would examine my finances. Make immediate adjustments. Don't wait. If I've got three cars now and I only need one, get rid of a couple of them.

I would suggest, naturally, that they come to places like us for help. And above all, they get started on their own.

Starting is a problem. I guess I'm speaking from bias. I see people now who are in financial trouble. I see people who could have come and signed up for our services months ago and are clamoring for it now. I see people who have really not done any job search because they thought they were going back. And the figures we hear is that it normally takes on an average, three months to find a job.

So if a person waits until they run out of everything and it takes them three months to find a job, they're in deep trouble.

I feel bad, you know. I think, too, there's so many people who don't know what to do. I think they need to develop a career plan. Maybe look at what skills do they have. I call it a market study. Rather than just go out and look for a job, try to develop a plan where you're targeting yourself. Maybe not just in one area, but in several areas. Reassess your skills and training.

A lot of people have skills they don't even know they have, that they acquired outside of General Motors that could be very useful.

I have a case, I won't mention the name, a man who's a millwright. I believe he's a journeyman. He's laid off. A millwright is a declining trade. Plus the only people that I understand use millwrights are big, industrial complexes. If GM is letting millwrights go, we have no other place to send them, locally.

This man graduated from a general engineering course in 1980, a four year degree. And apparently could not find a job then and went to work for GM. Then really never gave much thought to engineering again.

We talked. We have not yet been successful in placing him, but he's had two interviews as an entry level engineer.

And I'm saying it's rare to find an engineer in your blue-collar people, but it is not rare to find exceptional skills that maybe they were never able to use in General Motors.

I guess one thing, too, these people need to face is that many of them have never looked for a job. Some friend or relative gave them an application. They filled it out, turned it in. And they got a mysterious phone call saying, "Go take a physical and come to work next Monday."

The job market is competitive. Everybody out there—they can even be illiterate—will probably have a professional resume. If you don't have a resume, you are at an unfair [dis]advantage.

If you don't know how to conduct your search, and a lot of people in the job market have been taught this somewhat, you're at a disadvantage. Now, these are services we provide here. All voluntary, nobody has to do a thing.

But I'm saying, for many people, this is the job market you're competing in. Employers are very particular. They'll interview a number of people even for a minimum wage job, and pick out the person they feel is the best. Now, they're faced with a lot of turnover because of the wages. Still, they're looking for a top-notch person even if it's a rotten job.

I guess one thing I try to do with people is not to discourage them in any way. Because you don't need discouragement on top of this layoff. But you try to look at reality and say: Where do we go from here? Realistically.

Why do we send people to school? That's to get them a better skill so they can get a job. We are not here to support schools. It's beneficial to schools and I'm sure they're grateful. We're spending a lot of money with educational institutions.

But the real purpose of sending them there is to prepare them to go out in the world and make a living.

Career planning? We do it right here. We use the MOIS system, which is a state system. Typically, if you go anyplace else, that's what you use. I think the Genesee Intermediate School District, the Public Library has the MOIS system. I'm sure Mott College has it.

And these people have it available. Now, the library has counseling—I mean they have a resource center with a counselor on duty. I understand at Mott, they have a walk-in center where anybody can go in and take advantage of it.

And I think this is great because sometimes . . . let's take the person that's in a declining trade. The MOIS system might be good for that person to say, This is what I know, now how can I transfer to another area? Or by maybe, adding a few things to it, perhaps I can develop a new skill that will be acceptable out there.

One thing that concerns me is the psychological end, too, that these people have to go through. I say it is rejection to lose your job. When you are job hunting, you face a lot of rejection. I feel that there's a lot of emotional stress. And yet, to get a job, you almost *need* to feel good about yourself.

I mean, if you get to a point where you can't make your house payments, you're in danger of losing your house, and you've got to go on welfare—how are you going to go on a job interview?

I'm saying that you can spiral downward financially to a point where it's hard to get back up.

We are running into people already in deep financial trouble. See, some of these layoffs started a year ago. Plus, now I'm not an expert on the SUB-fund, but I guess the more people who are drawing and the higher their seniority, it dwindles faster. Which means these people thought: Boy, I'm okay for a while. And all of a sudden, they're not okay for as long as they thought they were going to be.

One thing that's tough to face is, really, nobody owes us a living. Okay. GM's not going to guarantee you a job. Nor any other employer. If the chips are down and it's a question of whether the boss loses his job or you, it's not going to be the boss.

I think that as a job developer and this would apply to counselors, too, you really have to be sensitive to these people. They're going through a lot of turmoil and they have to make a lot of adjustments.

I think one thing that's tough that I have thought about a lot, but if I had my choice of all the jobs in the world, I would not be a job developer.

I've been in this situation myself. First of all, I've gone through long-term unemployment twice where I really had to knock on a lot of doors. Where the going got rough. I think that's one thing that makes me a good job developer. Because I've been where these people are. Except by the grace of God, I made it, before I ran out of assets. I've been lucky.

But one thing that is really tough. Sometimes you get in this situation and you have left something good behind. You have to choose maybe not between a good choice and a bad choice, but between a mediocre and a rotten choice. Do you follow me?

So, your choices are not the best many times. And this makes it harder to make a decision and say, Hey, you know, I've got to adjust.

A couple observations I've made. One: I try and convey the idea to people: When you get a job, it's not over. You got a lot of people behind you here. If you hear of things, possible job opportunities, let us know. And I have probably several dozen people that have done that in spite of the fact they're working. Who have given us feedback and I think that's terrific—that people do care.

I think I tried to plant a seed; they might not have thought to do it if I hadn't mentioned it. So it's been real interesting to see that they have some concern. And I find this, too, in job clubs. When people get their jobs, they're really concerned about the people left behind that haven't achieved that yet.

I have told clients that I have placed, maybe not these exact words, but: I'm hired by the center, I'm really paid out of the nickel fund, which is something that you've contributed toward and GM matched. But if you went to a private employment agency, the service I have performed for you would have cost you three or four thousand dollars. And I just want you to know that you are getting a good service.

I'm trying to counteract the feeling that if it's free, it's no good.

And I guess my gut feeling as an outsider is that it's devastating to be a laid-off GM worker. But it's twice as devastating to be a non-GM laid-off worker because they do not have the same resources.

They interviewed some people on TV I remember seeing a fellow complaining because he wasn't going to get as much over-time. He used to make $60,000 and now he was only making $40,000 and he wonders how he's going to get along. And I wish that person could come in and meet some of these people. And he'd go back and say, "Boy, I'm lucky."

Lockrey

Vickie Lockrey, thirty-two, a rather small-boned woman with wispy, light brown hair, had been employed by General Motors at the AC Spark Plug Plant for almost nine years. She is now working at two part-time jobs. Her benefits—SUB-pay and unemployment—are almost depleted. She only recently entered the Human Resource Center's orientations.

Her plant, AC, is not closed. It has had a history of being one of the more stable plants, as far as layoffs are concerned.

I graduated in '73 and I worked five years in a restaurant as a waitress. I started working at Buick in 1978. When I got laid off I had almost nine years service altogether at General Motors.

I worked six years for Buick and then they went down for that model change for Buick City. We all went into the hiring pool. AC picked me up and Buick called me back around December of '85 and then, anyways, I decided that I wasn't going to go back to Buick.

I had it so good at AC because they had hired all these people off the street. That was in '85. If I would have gone back to Buick, I would have been on the bottom again. So I stayed at AC and then I got laid off a year later. I had almost two years seniority in that plant. It was in October of '86 when I got laid off so it's been a little over a year.

See, I was lucky, because they were taking one SUB-credit out of me a week. I collected eleven months, whereas most people now are collecting five and six months. So I was pretty lucky.

I didn't start going to the HRC until around . . . in the summertime. See, they told us we'd be going back in the spring. So, I didn't really look for a job or anything. Just set back and collected unemployment and SUB in the hope that I would go back.

The Resource Center contracted me. I didn't contact them. They asked me if I was interested in the job club and different things.

I didn't really start looking for a job until around July of '87.

I knew I wouldn't get called back to Buick, but I figured I'd be called back to AC because I'd been keeping in contact with the committeeman and they were getting my hopes up.

And still when I talked to them a couple of months ago, at contract time, they promised that—not really promised—but I was told that if the contract went through and things worked out the way they wanted it to that AC would be calling back some of the people.

And I'm not really that far from the cutoff date.

At the job center, they . . . they don't like you to talk about going back. They want us to face up and go on with our lives and start something new. But it's not that easy. It's really not.

It's very difficult because I had no skills. I still don't have any skills. I'm going back to school which I really didn't want to do because I don't enjoy it now, going back. But I feel that I have no choice.

I took a class in typing and word processing because everything is computers now and that's the demand. I figured, well, I'll try that and see how it works out. I've been looking for mostly factory work but they want to hire you through the temporary services so that the temporaries pay you the minimum wage and they make the money.

And it's hard to get in any of the factories.

I've got a half a dozen calls from the temporaries. I got one yesterday. I wouldn't mind working for them if they could work around my hospital schedule. I work part-time at St. Joe's as a housekeeper. But that's only maybe . . . we get paid every two weeks. This pay period I will get a five-day pay and that's for two weeks. So that's not very much. I average about $500 a month and my bills come to about $900 a month and I'm living partially off my savings account. I can get by maybe until the middle of summer and then I have to decide what to do. To sell my house or something.

I might have to end up moving back home which I really don't want to have to do.

I had a baby-sitting job during the afternoons, but that interfered with the hospital work because the days I couldn't sit, she had to get somebody else. And they had two or three different sitters all the time, so she finally got somebody permanent. I was knocked out of that job.

Which I could understand because it is hard to get somebody and then have two or three people baby-sit your kids.

But I still sit at night. You know, somebody calls, they want me to watch their kids. I'll drop everything just for that extra five bucks. (Laughs.) Because it's gas in my car. I used to be able to turn that down.

I also work for a woman cleaning dentists' offices. She had me working like two or three days a week at first but now it's only one day a week. So you go in there, maybe, ten dollars for the night and that's it.

But you know, this money, it adds up. Each month I figure I'm earning probably an extra hundred, hundred and fifty dollars just from these.

I had a week's notice when I got laid off. But there had been rumors. We knew we were getting laid off because every week a bulletin would go up and say how many people were getting laid off that Friday.

We knew because they were laying off every two weeks. There was a list of people.

But you don't have time to prepare for this. You know, it's like they were doing so good the year before that. I mean, really good. All the shops were hiring people. We thought, Well, finally, it's about time they started bringing new people in here. Move us up a little seniority-wise.

And then, all of a sudden, it just started going downhill.

I know there's still a lot of people who have accepted it. But like, for me, my plant hasn't closed. And they don't plan on closing at least within the next three years and they are doing things to try to build up work, to try to create more jobs.

So I'm still hanging onto that one thread of hope.

I'm still planning but I'm hoping that I don't have to change careers.

Because no matter what, even if I do get into an office and I do have a different job where I'm working full-time and making money, it's still not going to match GM.

I don't want a job where I'm making $13 an hour necessarily, but even now, for me, I'd have to be making at least $7 or $8, just to get by.

And what I miss is being able to save money. Being able to put it away. I can't do that anymore. All I can do is take it out.

Just to get by. A lot of places call but they don't want to work around the hospital schedule. That's what's difficult. I would be willing to work part-time somewhere else for minimum wage. That would really help me out. But they will not work around the hospital. They want you when they want you. It just doesn't work out that way.

And I don't know how . . . there's some people that do it and I don't know how. I have a feeling that I might have to find another part-time job this summer. I'm not going to school this summer.

But I just . . . I don't know, I can't visualize . . . I keep looking at the bad side. Knowing that, no matter what, I'm going to lose my house. There's no way I can keep it. I don't think I'll be able to ever own a home again or a brand new car.

I'm hoping that my truck will last me a couple years but the way the cost of living is, you just can't . . . Even on $800 a month you're just barely making it.

I looked into an apartment and they cost more than my house. And it's just ridiculous. I mean you can't . . . It's being able to live. It's not as much the job, it's being able to survive with the way things are.

And then these companies, they know that most of these people are begging for jobs so it's like, Well, we can work them minimum wage, we don't have to work them for any more than that because they're so desperate. We're going to take the jobs and they know it. That's why they go through these temporaries services.

A lot of these shops were not hiring through these temporaries a couple of years ago. Because I know friends who were working in some of these factories, making like six, seven dollars an hour. And they're telling me, Put in an application.

And I did. When I got called, they said, "Well, you have to go down to the temporary place and then we call them." Because they don't have to pay the benefits; the temporaries are the ones that have to take care of all the benefits and raises and all this. And the company doesn't have to.

Well, some of the temporaries now will work around a schedule. Like, Victor Temporaries will work around your schedule. But what you have to do is, on the days you know you're going to be off, you tell them you're available.

And I did that for about a month and then I decided this is ridiculous. Because I had to sit by the phone and wait to see if they were going to call me for a job and this would be maybe just one night. Like, somebody called in sick somewhere so they call you and say, Can you come in and go work at such-and-such a place.

I got tired of it because—I have an answering machine, but if you want to go somewhere and they call you and you're not home, well, they have to know that you're going to be there.

I had one employer call me from Flint Coating and he was mad. He would have hired me. A friend of mine worked there and I put in a resume and the friend told him about me. He brought the resume in for me.

Well, he had a job opening. He said they were going through the temporaries.

I said, Well, fine, but I hadn't signed up with the temporary they were going through. But he wanted me that next day. I said, "I can work Monday, but I have to sit today and tomorrow. Can't I start Monday?"

He said, "Well, we'll talk about this later. Just go down and sign up and then give me a call." Well, I couldn't go down that morning and he called me the next morning and he said, "I want you today." He said, "Can you work for me today?" And I said, "No, but I can start Monday." He said, "Forget it." He hung up on me. He was mad.

But I was told that if you're working for them and you're going to another job, they want notice. They want to know. They don't want you to say, Well, I'm not coming in tomorrow, because I've got another job. They don't see it your way.

And I was told by the Human Resource Center and several others that if they couldn't wait . . . he didn't get anybody until that next week anyway. He said, "I thought you needed a job really bad." I said, "I do, but I cannot go in today."

I had kids with me that day when he called. I had kids with me. I couldn't just run over, pick them up and haul them.

I told him, "I have kids, I can't just pick up and leave." I told him I was sitting. He said, "Well, when's their parents coming home?" I told him it would be late in the afternoon, but then I had another sitting job I had to go to after that. And he just didn't understand so he got somebody else.

He figured I didn't need a job bad enough because I didn't drop everything right then and go down there. And usually, when employers call for an interview, they let me set up an appointment. I'll tell them I'm available in the mornings or in the afternoon. And then they'll set a time and say, Is that all right?

But I'm kind of glad I didn't work for him. I was told later that very few people stay on this job he wanted me to go on.

He'll show you the job. If you can't learn it within so many days, you're out the door. They don't give you another chance.

But at General Motors, if you can't learn a job, they'll take you to a different job. In fact, that was what happened with me. The very first day I hired in the shop, I could not do the job they gave me and I was black-and-blue all over.

I mean, I was black-and-blue—my arms, my legs—because I'd lean up against the car with my leg to steady myself and then I'd lean with my arm on the car door. And I was just so sore.

They were going to fire me. The foreman wanted to let me go but they couldn't do it. They had to give me another chance. That's one good thing about the union. You can't just boot somebody out the door.

All these small factories are at an advantage right now because they can pay the lower wages and they know there's desperate people, especially factory workers, that would be willing to work for them.

It's like they have their pick of people. Like I was telling my dad. Let's say there was a turnaround and GM was hiring all these people back. You watch. The wages would go up. These businesses would be begging for people. And they probably would hire for more than minimum wage.

If I was married and had somebody to bring with me, to relocate to another state, it would be different. But my family's here and just to go out and do something, you know, be by myself not knowing anybody—it's just really hard. And I don't think I'd want to do it.

If I had a spouse who was laid off or he wanted to move, that'd be different. And I know a lot of people feel the same way. They asked us that in the job club. Would you be willing to relocate? There was a couple of other women who were single, whose families were here. They didn't want to go somewhere by themselves and just start over again.

I think I'd be more depressed because I wouldn't have anybody to talk to. I couldn't just call up my mom and I'm really close to my two nephews. They're like my own kids. I couldn't love them any more if they were my own. And not to be able to see them. I don't think I could handle that.

(Sighs.) Well, in the job club, we just get together. There's . . . it's usually one to two hours a week. I think they have it twice a week now. And we get together, compare notes, and give each other leads.

Let's say there's somebody who's a welder and they're trying to find a job. And maybe you're not looking for a welding job but you know somebody that's hiring for one. You can go to the club and say, I know an employer who needs a welder. You give them the address and tell them where they can go. Or maybe they know some factories or some place for you.

Like, I had a lead on that Femco Factory that went up. I put a resume in there but then the paper said it was for the people skilled in plastics. So, right then, I thought, I haven't got a chance. And I think they were paying like $6.50 an hour starting pay.

And I thought that'd be great. Because what I need is full time, benefits. There's just so many things. You know, I have no health insurance right now and to pay, just for me, once a month it would be quite expensive. If I had kids I'd be paying it. But just for me I feel I'd be paying too much.

One lady who works at St. Joe's part-time, I think she said it's over a hundred dollars a month and I thought for me, that'd be really expensive.

I could have continued it through General Motors but even then ... I just couldn't see paying that much money. I'm just hoping I never have to go to the hospital. I get a discount if I'm still working for St. Joe's but still the bills would be humungous.

It'd take me forever to pay it back. They'd have to deduct it out of my check. (Laughs.)

I have my foot in the door for St. Joe's because a lot of people start out in housekeeping and move up. You have to be there for six months before you can apply for an outside job in the hospital. I think it's six months.

But they pay good money. I could probably live off $6.00 an hour. I wouldn't be able to save any money, but at least I would be able to pay my bills. But over there, you know, they'd rather work you part-time than full-time. And that's everywhere now.

I mean, it's almost impossible to get full-time unless you are working minimum wage.

And you have to be there a year or more before you can even get full-time. Even to be considered for it and that's a drawback.

See, maybe in the future, something's going to come up but what are we supposed to do now? See, now is the important thing.

They told me at the Human Resource Center, "Well, why didn't you start looking for a job when you were first laid off? Why didn't you start school as soon as you got laid off?" I said, "Because I didn't want to." I didn't. I didn't. I've gotten laid off a hundred times and I've always went back.

It didn't really bother me this time. It was something I was putting off because I did not want to do it. I didn't want to have to go through all that. But then, they keep saying, Well, don't let your benefits run out, don't wait around.

But it still takes time. You know, it still takes time to have to retrain or to acquire a skill. And most places you can't just go out and say, Well, I've got a degree. They don't care if you've got a degree. They want experience: Well, did you work doing this? Have you done this?

The only jobs you can get are maybe through the temporaries to acquire the experience. They'll hire you, but then how are you supposed to live?

I figure for the next two years I'm going to be struggling if I don't get called back. Because it's going to be a while. You can't just go to school and acquire a skill and then go out there and start a new career. Unless maybe you've had some background before that.

See, there's a lot of people that just know the shop and nothing else. And I never even thought about going back to school or anything when I was working in the shop. Because I thought, Why should I go back to school to acquire a skill that's going to pay less money than what I'm making now?

And that's the attitude of a lot of people. It's different if you get into your business or maybe you had a skill before you got in the shop. There's some people that had skills before they got in the shop. There's people who quit good jobs to go work in the shop because it paid more money.

But they still cannot find work now.

I took a typing test for medical billing. I'm just starting out in typing, but HRC talked me into taking this test. I told them I didn't think I was ready. And they insisted that, you know, what could it hurt? Take it anyway.

I did pretty good as far as the words per minute, but it was the errors. I'm not at the point yet where I can type without making a lot of mistakes.

Now in class, I don't like my instructor. He treats us like we're high school kids; he does not like people, period. I don't know what he's doing there teaching because he definitely does not like people. He deliberately humiliates people in front of the class. And me not wanting to go to school in the first place and having to come and face that every day, you know.

I almost dropped out. I almost said forget it because I just . . . I go in there and I'd get really nervous during tests. And he'd make it hard. It was like he expected more than what we could do. I don't like having to go back to school and be treated like a high school kid.

I feel like I'm going back and starting over again and have to make a decision on what I'm going to do when I get older! (Laughs.) It's really hard.

At this point I don't even feel like I have a future. I don't know, I go to school and I get discouraged. I passed all my classes, but I really didn't think I was going to make it through those.

See, I didn't enjoy taking the class. Now, my sister was taking adult night classes at the high school and she loved it and she was doing really good. She was doing better than me. And she just loved it because her instructor made it fun. He didn't push. But our instructor . . . We had a test one day. And he said we had five minutes to prepare. He told us what page, you know, get out our papers. Well, I asked the girl next to me a question. It didn't have anything to do with the test. I just asked her a simple question.

And he said to me, "Have the rules changed, Miss Lockrey?" and I said, "I don't know what you're talking about. What rules?" he said, "The test rules." And I said, "What are you getting at? What's your point?"

He said, "There's no talking during a test." I said, "I understood the test is not started yet. You told us we had five minutes." He said, "It doesn't matter. As soon as you walk into this class, you do not talk to your neighbor."

I mean, he treats us like a bunch of little kids, like we're elementary kids. He'll go and watch people; he'll stand by them while they're typing if they're doing a problem. He just sits there and he makes you feel so small.

Somebody wondered if he was married and said they felt sorry for his wife. But you know, usually, people like that, the wife dominates them and they come to work . . . (Laughs.) Because I've known a case like that.

I was working at Buick there with a supervisor like that. He was that type. He liked to dominate people, you know, be really tough. Well, somebody saw him with his wife one time. And when he was with his wife, he was this meek little man. (Laughs.) And I say, that's the problem, they have to prove themselves outside of the home.

But I've got this guy for next semester and I don't know how I'm going to get through it. Nobody does it in the mornings, just him. He's the only instructor.

Oh, he does depress you. I'd go home and sit there and I'd cry. Because I thought I just can't take this, you know. He just made my day even worse. I'd already be depressed and then I'd go home and I'd start thinking.

Well, I'd go there and then I'd go to the job club and they're saying, Face up to the fact that you're not going to back to work. You're not ever getting called back and then I just feel so depressed. I'd go home and I'd think . . . I just can't take this. I hated going to school.

Even now. I have to start Monday. I dread it. But I know if I don't go, then I'm just going to be sitting back, cleaning toilets the rest of my life if I don't go back. So it's like you have no choice.

But there's another drawback, too, to getting another job. It's the one dreaded question: *If you get called back, will you go back to GM?* And I don't think it's fair.

At the Human Resource Center, they're trying to tell us how to get around this. And they say, "Well, you tell them that your plant is closed." And I say, "But my plant isn't closed." and they say, "Well, they don't know that."

But an employer knows that you're not going to sit there and say, No, I'm not going back. For me, I don't care where I'm at. I'd go back. Unless, let's say, I lost my recall rights and I would have had to start seniority all over again with General Motors and I'm making enough money where I can survive and maybe save a little. Then I would reconsider about going back.

But to give up nine years seniority or service time. And to give up $13 an hour. There's no way.

It's been over a year for a lot of people. Especially when you tell employers, "I've been laid off for over a year," they think, Well, gee, she's been laid off this long, I don't think she's going back.

But like, sure, Fisher Body. If I had come from Fisher Body, which closed, or even Buick City, I wouldn't be going back.

See, at Buick I'd be on the bottom of getting called back. They're going to start up second shift in March. They said most of those people will go back to work. But because of the Fisher people coming over, the low seniority won't be going back.

And with me, my seniority, I would have had nine years service, my chances would have been very slim because I would have been on rock bottom. But at AC there's like, maybe, a little under nine hundred people laid off over at AC. And I'm toward the top. I'm not at the bottom, I'm not in the middle, I'm more toward the top. So, I think if they even called back only two hundred people, I think I would be in that group.

I talked to the committeeman when Buick called me back and I asked him what he thought. He said, "Well, there's a lot of people under you." At the time I think there was like seven hundred people under me. If I would have went to Buick City, there wouldn't have been anybody.

They don't have anybody under nine years over at Buick. And right now AC's got three and a half seniority.

But see, I was willing to take a wage cut. They were talking about taking wage cuts.

When I talked to the committeeman, I said, "Why don't they let us?" I said, "If taking a wage cut is going to give me my job back, I'd rather be making seven dollars, eight dollars an hour than to be making minimum wage. At least getting my benefits." And he said, "Oh no, no, we will not do that." And I said, "But why? Why shouldn't it be up to us?"

I would take a wage cut. If it's going to save my job, if it's going to get me back to work, I'd be willing to take a wage cut. Not a drastic one, you know, where we're just going to be fighting to survive.

There's ways around it, but the union has its advantages but it's got its disadvantages. Because the union is partially the reason why we're out of a job, too. Because they're stubborn.

But of course, the people that are working that don't have to worry about it, they're going to say no, too.

They're still working overtime right now. They said they were going to cut that.

My aunt was telling my dad about how the mutual retirement provision in the contract went through for AC and that some people went out in December and then I guess a bunch more go out in March or something.

And my mom said, "Do they plan to replace them?" And she said, "They're trying to get around it." They agreed to it in the contract, but I knew they'd try to get out of it.

Because if they did replace fifty percent there's no reason why most of us couldn't get back in to work.

And my mom asked her, "Well, how many went out?" And she said, "I don't know, I don't keep track." See, if they're working, they don't care about us. They don't care.

Now, my mom read an article the other night. I don't get the paper and she cut it out for me. I told her, "Save all the good news." Ha! And I've got articles. I read them and it kind of helps a little, getting me out of a depression.

But she said that there was an article on AC doing good and that they were trying to create more jobs. That's what I don't understand. If they are, why can't they bring some of us back? Why do they have to keep rotating, keeping the same people?

I realize it's to save money, but it's like they just don't care about us. They don't care.

The union says they're for us, they're trying to get us back. I talked to a couple of union guys, "Yeah, we're trying to get you back. We're doing everything we can."

But I just don't see them doing that. I don't really think they are. I really don't think they're working hard enough to get us back because they're letting too many things happen.

I was told, Well, if that retirement goes through and if we can get the contract like Ford and they have to replace fifty, you'll be getting called back. And now, all I'm hearing is they don't want to, they don't have to.

I just don't understand. They say car sales are down, but it's not car sales. They're using that as an excuse. GM's doing good. They're making profits.

But they're using everything they can and they're legally getting away with it. That's the reason they agreed to this contract because they knew they'd find loopholes where they can get around everything.

They have never honored a contract, yet. I mean, they've broken things. They've always ended up getting around things that would be to their benefit and not ours. Like the profit-sharing and different things. They've always gotten around all this.

Like the first year, sure, it was good. We're all, Oh, wow, we got $300 and something dollars. The first year we got it and the last two years—nothing.

And then they made all kinds of excuses why we didn't get it. Oh, yeah (laughs wryly), I've got a lot of advice for the company!

I envy the people that have spouses—have somebody—especially if there's another income coming in.

I've talked to a lot of my friends who are married. They're working part-time but still getting benefits from their husbands' job. And they're not really worried about it. They're not going to school. They don't care. It's more or less, they're taking a vacation. And they're not really worried.

A lot of these women that did get in the shop, it's more or less they're married, they have a husband who's working.

They're not really worried. Well, fine, so I have to take a cut in pay. I'll go out and get a new career and do something else. It's more or less they got in the shop to get a job and help with the bills. But for me I'm sole supporter.

Or they're so used to the two incomes that they can't get along without the other.

But most of the people in the job club—the women—are not married, they're single. Not too many of the married ones are going there. In fact, most of them are really low, low seniority people or ones whose plants have closed. There's a couple from AC that were going to the job club but they were new hires, just hired off the street. So it's like they haven't really invested their time into General Motors.

I'm the only one there who's got the nine years service. And I'm still sitting there, believing that I'm going back to work. Still hoping and they're all shaking their heads and they're all saying, I don't want to go back. And I know that if they got that call, they'd be out the door. They'd be going.

But I guess maybe that's what they're doing to keep themselves going. Is to face up to the fact that . . . like I said, new hires. Maybe got a couple years at the shop and then got laid off.

I envy their ambition, their wanting to get out and start something new. It's like they've already given up and said, Okay, we're going to do this or that. And I guess I just don't have that—that ambition, or feeling. I'm still hanging on, hoping that something's going to happen.

And everybody I talk to, even people who don't work in the shop, if I even mention going back, they're shaking their heads and are saying, You're never going back.

My mom's always saying, I read it in the paper where things look really bad. I've talked to so and so and she said . . .

But it's not impossible. That's what makes me mad. It's not impossible for things to . . . It's General Motors. They're the ones that are . . . They have the control. They're the ones that are keeping us out. I know there's ways of getting us back to work.

There are jobs. There's things they can do. They just don't want to.

I mean, sure, they're closing all these plants. When they've got like three thousand people on the street because they've closed the plant, they're not going to be able to distribute them and get them all jobs. But I can't see them keeping everybody out.

I'm sure the union, they're doing things. They talk about doing things, but you don't see anything happening. Like it's all talk. No action is being taken.

See, I tried calling yesterday. I asked to talk to Sam Isaac. He's usually the one I talk to. The secretary, she . . .

And now I wish I hadn't said anything to her. Because I asked if I could speak to him and she said, "He's not in, but could I have your name and number and I'll have him call you back." And I said, "Fine." She said, "Can I give him a message? What do you want to ask him?" And I said, "Oh, I just would like some information about work." And she said, "What plant are you from?" And I said, "I'm not, I'm laid off." She said, "Oh." As soon as I told her I was laid off, her tone changed and everything. I knew right then that I blew it.

"Well, maybe you want to talk to somebody else. Why don't you call back tomorrow?" I said, "No, I'd like to talk to Sam Isaac."

She said, "Well, no, I think Don Hobson could give you more information." Well, I've talked to him before and he is really vague about what's going on. And she said, "He's the head of the mutual retirement thing and he would know more about it."

I said, "Well, I just want to find out if they plan on replacing those retirees." I said, "I want to know what they're going to do about it." Sam Isaac told me that when the retirees went out they were going to replace them. He said, "You call me back in a couple more months and I'll keep you informed about what's going on."

And I knew I wasn't going to get a call back from him.

So I thought, Well, maybe I'll give him a call today. But you can't get past the secretary. I've even walked down there. And she'll sit there, "Well, I'll give you the information you need." You can't get past those secretaries. They don't want you to talk to them.

And I think the committeeman probably said, "If they want to talk about work . . ." I'm sure they get a lot of calls from the laid-off employees.

I should have just said it's personal and I'd like to talk to him. Because he did call me one time. A friend of mine that was still working there, she contacted him and said, "Will you please call her?" And he called me.

He said, "I've had your phone number for a while and something told me to call you. A friend told me to call you, but it's been on my conscience that I should call you." And it really got my hopes up, just talking to him.

But you never know anymore if they're just trying to keep you happy so you won't keep bothering them. Or how much of it is true and how much of it isn't. I just don't know.

I wish I knew somebody who really knew what was going on there. I want a yes or no. I want a definite answer. Am I going back or am I not? I don't like this waiting and this hoping. Like I told him, "If there's no chance of me going back, don't sit there and lie to me." I said, "I don't want to hear lies. I have to know."

If I'm going to go for on-the-job training, I don't want to train for a new job and then get a letter from GM and all this training is just . . . They're going to be mad at me if I do all this training and then GM calls me back.

But that's another thing. In the contract, they're supposed to increase the benefits and I don't see any of that. Increase the benefits so that people could be laid off longer and still collect more. They were trying to get an extension on the unemployment but that never went through.

They were talking about TRA. Now, there's a few people who qualify for TRA that came from Chevy Plant. Trade Readjustment Act. That's if your job is lost due to foreign trade, things like that. I was hoping I would be under that, but at AC, that's not really why people lost jobs. It hasn't been through foreign trade.

Well, I looked for an AC filter and I couldn't find one. Only one store and that was so high, I couldn't afford it. I had to go get a different one for an air filter, because nobody sells AC products anymore. You used to be able to go in a store and find AC products. No, they're going to FRAMM and oh, I forgot the other type.

And they're about five dollars, six dollars cheaper.

And they're gaining contracts but they're losing and they're not gaining any more. One line will go down and another will start up. Like they're just moving people around and they're mot getting ahead enough where they can hire people back. They're just staying the same.

And I keep thinking something's gotta' give. They've either gotta' lay off or hire back or something. I'm afraid it's going to go down so far they're going to have to let people go rather than to bring them back. That's what I'm afraid of.

If they could just get something in there. You'd think they could at least make something else.

I think what'll end up happening is maybe somebody outside of GM will buy the plant. Even so. Let's say somebody outside GM buys the plant and starts making parts. Maybe five dollars, six dollars an hour.

But I think GM should make it so that, fine, you buy the plant but let our people have first choice of working there before you call in somebody else. Make an arrangement so that our people have a chance first.

Now, I have a friend who works at Chevrolet Truck. In fact, he's going back in two weeks and I'll be getting his kids off to school in the morning so that'll help me money-wise. I'll be getting about $30 a week just for getting them off to school.

He said that they're going to have to let go of about six hundred people when all these voluntarily laid-off people go back. They were hoping they could keep them but I guess they can't. So he said they'll be letting go about six hundred. But he said that there are rumors that they're going to start a line back up and put something else in there. And that would bring those people back.

I've been hearing that, too, for a couple of years. But when you talk to people in management or somebody, they say, "No, I haven't heard nothing." They don't want to talk about it.

He said they're putting a new truck in there and everything. So why would they remodel if they're not planning on putting anything in there? Why would they just leave it idle? Unless they plan on moving things around. Now, sometimes they'll do that.

I had an offer to go to Pontiac but all the high seniority took the jobs and then they only needed one hundred thirty people. Last I heard they only moved forty of them and then they waited a whole year.

I know some of the Buick people moved to Pontiac, too. I talked to a woman who went. She said, "Yeah, our plant's closing this week." But she heard it was temporary. But she wasn't sure. She said you hear things, but they don't really say. She said they said the closing was only for six months and then they would get it going again. She wasn't sure.

You hear that all the time and then nothing happens.

For a while there, I was sorry I didn't go down there and then when I hear about that, I was sorry I didn't go back to Buick for a while because they were going really good. When I got laid off, they were going strong.

You're think to yourself, Maybe I should have done this or that.

Now I'm in a situation where I feel that the decision I made was probably the best out of any of them so far. Because I have a better chance of going back to AC than I would have of going back to any of these other plants.

But as far as giving up completely that I'll be called back to GM, I mean, I refuse. I don't care what anybody says. I refuse to give up.

Because once we do that we're saying, Okay, fine, go ahead, you know, let it happen. Something has to be done. If we just all sit back and accept it then they're getting what they wanted.

You know, they're getting away with it.

But we need the support of the people that are working, too. Not just the laid-off workers. We need everybody. It's like, the ones that are working, that do have their jobs that are secure. They don't care.

They'll say, "Oh, yeah, I might not have a job in five years either," but it's not really bothering them until they're on the street.

And we need everybody to support us, not just a few. Not just the laid-off workers. We need everybody.

You know, if they could just at least get the people that have got the time in, that have invested their time. When contract talks were going on, instead of trying to keep the people they already had, why didn't they try to get us back, too?

I can see, so, they don't want to ever hire anybody off the street again, whatever. Fine. But keep the people they've already got. Try to keep us in there. We've built our life around this place. And then they're just kicking us out in the street and saying, "Find a new career. Go back to school." Well it's not that simple just going back to school and finding a new career. But some people just love going back to school. They just love it.

Now, for me, I was always very careful. People always said, You can afford this, and you can afford that. But I always saved my money. And even when I was working at General Motors, I never took my job for granted.

I always made sure I saved. I counted my checks every week to make sure that if I got laid off, I'd have twenty-six weeks in to collect unemployment.

GM knew about this way ahead of time. They knew about it. I know they did. They knew. And they don't care. That's what hurts. They don't care. I feel it's terrible. All these people out of jobs, out of work, and they just don't care about them. They're rich. It's not bothering them.

I was thinking, If I could win the lottery, if I could win a lot of money, I would put in a fund especially for the laid-off workers. I would. I mean, honest to God, I would, because I feel that they deserve something.

11

Ellis

Faith Ellis's bubbly personality carried her through two layoffs. She has been through the Human Resource Center twice, and most recently was placed in on-the-job training as an electrician trainee.

She is thirty-three, with large blue eyes and curly brown hair, and has two small sons.

I've worked for GM for about four years. I started out at Manufacturing downtown Flint. The old Chevrolet. They called it "the hole."

You know how it is in the shop. You always hear rumors that they're going to be getting laid off. I thought I wasn't even going to get a year in down there. That was the rumors going around down there, you know, *You're not going to make it, you're not going to get your year* and I thought I was going to get laid off.

Instead of getting laid off I was sent to another plant. So I stayed up until '79, August '79, which I was one of the lucky ones to stay that long.

From Truck and Bus, I went to work there in October '85, and I got laid off there June 5 of '87.

I knew when I hired in that I wasn't going to be there a long time. There were rumors going around that they were going to close the plant. And I think they were just putting the second shift back on to get the trucks out in the amount of time that they were required to have them out. So they called all these people back in knowing that we weren't going to be there forever.

A lot of people at the other plants were more fortunate. They got to stay longer but I wasn't one of the lucky ones and ended up going out the door.

Well, see, I was on ADC for a while. And I decided, you

know, come hell or high water, that I wasn't ever going to go back on that.

No matter what. If I had to go to work at a Sunshine or wherever I was not going back on those ADC lines.

The only thing that helped me was being on ADC. I did not want to go back to that. That bothered me to no end. I mean, that just . . . some people can handle that kind of life. I don't want to.

Being on ADC made me feel like I was less of a person. I didn't like feeling that way.

To stand in line to get food stamps or to go to the store and hand out food stamps. When I did that before I wanted to crawl underneath the table. I didn't want people to see me handing those food stamps to the cashier. I did my shopping at night just so nobody would see me.

And if I felt that way at that time, now would be worse. And I've pretty much always worked.

I worked all over. I worked as a waitress when I was younger about sixteen, seventeen. I didn't like that. I got married right away. And I went to Europe and I lived over in Germany and I started working at the commissary, which was a food center for the GIs.

But then I got divorced from my husband and came back to the States.

I went to Maine and I stayed up there for a while and found out I was pregnant and then I came back here [to the Flint area]. But in the meantime my ex-husband wasn't sending me any money. I mean zilch. I had quit my job so I had that thirteen-week extension of unemployment.

Here I was, getting fat, and I didn't have any money and no maternity clothes. He wouldn't send anything home. So I thought, What am I going to do?

I ended up going down to the Red Cross. And I had to get maternity clothes through the Red Cross. Yeah, I was down and out. And I didn't know . . . At that time I didn't know where my next meal was going to come from. I had to really scrape.

And I went down and I applied for Social Services there. And finally then, my unemployment came through so I got that. And I came back here.

So this time when I got laid off, I looked all over for jobs. And I didn't worry about it so much. I guess I figured with a lot of pushing and a lot of looking, I was going to find something.

I didn't worry. I didn't really worry about it.

Just about three weeks before I was going to lose my unemployment (laughs) I found out about this electrician training job.

141

But I guess I just had my mind set that I was going to find something and I had determination. And that's all it was.

Right after I got laid off I started looking. So that was from June until November 23rd.

I had thought about being a stewardess. HRC had an opening for that and I could get the training. They were going to send me up north. And the more I thought about it—it was great if you'd been married. You know, the money wouldn't have been bad and you would be home every night.

But money-wise, alone, I just couldn't make it. Not being a single parent. I have two boys: I've got one that's fifteen and one that is nine.

When we got laid off, they had a program right there at the building at General Motors. And so I went down. I listened to what they had to offer. Of course, I had been through the same program before when I got laid off. So I knew a little what it was about.

It was an orientation. They were telling me what you had to do and what you had to go through. And I thought, if they're still offering this, I got a job the last time. I said, I'm going to go again. So, that was my decision right there.

I know a lot of people down there. They were afraid. They thought, Well, I'll get called back, I'm going to wait and let my unemployment run out, I'm going to let my benefits run out. You know, *I'm going to wait*, yeah.

They wait until after they run out of all this . . . You would not believe all the people that were calling HRC. That were laid off about the same time I was. They were so booked down at HRC that they had to make reservations, they were so packed with people.

But they were swamped even before that. They were having a hard time with reservations, you know, for the orientation. Well, why didn't these people do this before?

People were waiting and thinking . . . But I guess maybe because I'd been in that spot before, I did something. I did because I looked at all these people that were going to be getting laid off and that made my chances of finding a job less the longer I waited.

I wasn't going to take that chance.

I even feel now that if I hadn't gotten this job with Ron that I probably would still be out looking for a job. Through HRC. I had been going to that job club there and every Thursday I would go in and I was looking for work and, of course, I had been out looking.

I had even traipsed through the mud at one place looking for a job. They didn't even have the building all up. I traipsed through mud. I had a couple inches thick of mud on me and I went up and I looked around.

And finally, I saw some guy and I asked, "Who can I talk to about finding a job here?" And he said, "Well, I really don't know." And I said, "Well, boy, this place is going up quick. I want to find out something." He said, "I really can't help you." So I went ahead and I looked at the sign of the company that was building the plant. And I thought, Well, gee, they might know something because they have to be dealing with them.

So I looked in the phone book and called information and they said, "Well, it's in Grand Blanc but they've got a Flint listing." I called there and she said, "All you have to do is bring a resume."

I dropped my resume off and I was back once a week and, of course, they knew me. All places knew me. I even went back to my old boss and I talked to him. I said, "Do you need some drivers?" He said no.

I talked to people. You know, you talk to people and anybody who might know somebody that needs some help. I was willing to learn.

And so I just went all over looking for jobs. And then I went to HRC every Thursday and they kept on coming up with something. But nothing that fit me because I didn't have the education.

I had a high school diploma. Of course, I'd taken nursing, you know, nursing assistant's training and I went back and I took a ward clerk training class. Just to kind of get the feel of, maybe . . . Is this the field that I want to go into?

Well, it wasn't. Definitely wasn't. Not after losing two patients.

So anyway, then Dave Rhodes called me. He said, "Faith, I found you a job." He knows I like a job where I'm active, where I'm doing something all the time.

And he said, "I've got something that might interest you. It's electronics. You've always talked about how you liked something that keeps you moving or where you're busy, something that's not repetitious."

And I said, "What is it?"

He said, "It's an electrical job, a training program. And we get you on-the-job training." I thought about it. At first I was going to turn it down. Just lack of confidence. This scary feeling of Gee, can I pick this stuff up? I don't know anything about electricity. The most I've ever used is a screwdriver and a hammer, you know. And my biggest downfall was my math.

My math was so poor. It still is. And to even use a ruler, I had no knowledge of the things like that. I never had to. And when I was growing up, you get married, you have a man to take care of you and things have changed since then. You know, we don't necessarily need them.

I thought, well, heck, after a couple of days of tossing and turning, I said go for it. Quit sitting back and saying, You can't do this, and you can't do that—go for it. Learn all you can learn.

And I still, to this day, have to keep saying to myself, Keep going, Faith, keep going.

Because of the lack of confidence. And my biggest downfall is math. I don't know it that well. Gloria [co-worker] is excellent at it. She knows everything. Yeah, she didn't at one time.

There was two of us that came over from HRC. I guess we both had an interview that day, so I went there. And I was a little bit scared because I thought she had the apprenticeship. She'd been with General Motors. She had a background in college. I don't know if she had her bachelor's or what and I thought, Oh, she's going to have the job. You know, she's worked in skilled trades in the shop and she's got everything that would be beneficial to this job.

So I was certain I didn't have it.

But I went out there and I talked to him. And I was a little scared because it didn't offer benefits and I just . . . I told Ron, I want the job. And I knew he was going to interview her. So then he had to ask Gloria, he said, Well, which one do you like?

Gloria said, "I don't know." She said, "I like them both." She said, "I kind of like Faith because she talks, you know. Just seems friendly." So then the next thing you know, I just called Ron and said, "Well, I'm interested in the job." He said, "Well, you can start just as soon as we get the paperwork done." So that was it.

It's not bad at all. No benefits. Not at this point. But that's one of Ron's top priorities is getting benefits. And I figure for a small business.

Okay, my first day. (Laughs.)

It was about a week and a half later, 'cause I had gone hunting and so after my hunting trip I started working. And I went in.

And the first day they had these big panels there. And Ron said, "Oh, you're just in time, we're going to be moving these panels out." And I thought, Oh, no. And Gloria had to leave in about an hour or so. And they were bringing these trucks in to load the panels on.

I didn't know anything about moving these big things. I was afraid it was going to fall on me. So that was most of my first day, moving these things in and out of the trucks. It was different.

Yeah, I got the muscles the first day I was there.

From that I think Ron showed me blueprint readings and of course, it didn't look like anything to me but just a bunch of lines going every which way.

You watch. I mostly watch Gloria because Gloria is usually the one who's always doing the panels. I watch her. I ask questions. And then as she did something, I'd go back to the print and say, Oh, that's what this is. And then I go back to her and see what she's doing next. Then I go back to the blueprint again.

But still, it's not all in my mind yet. I'm still—still really learning and I've got a lot of questions that are on the blueprints.

I've worked there since November 23rd and it's now January 8.

He was talking something today—about resistance, I think is what it was called. I'm not even sure of the name of it now. And he's talking way above my head, you know. But I listen. I try to pick it up, but I don't want to confuse myself, either, because there is so much and I can get so much going through my head at one time and you can't absorb everything you hear at once. You can't. You'd like to.

Well, print-wise, yes, I think it will all sink in. It has, with the blueprints: Oh, yeah, I remember him talking about this. I even listen to Gloria sometimes as they're talking about a panel that they built and how they did it and the wiring. And I think, How does she remember that wiring, you know? How does she remember? She really does. It's amazing. I think, Well, maybe in time I'll be able to do that, too.

Once you work with them so much you know what something is and you know what it's doing. And me, I'm curious as can be about: What's this do? How does it go up from here? What's an input and an output?

And rather than asking all these questions, I should be learning right now how they go in, where they go. And things like measuring, and later, once I get the blueprint reading down, and how to do the measuring. Then I think that will come along, as to what things are and how they work.

I'm going back to school, starting another blueprint reading class in February. I'm just taking that right now through the Mott Adult Continuing Education. Electrical blueprint reading and I'm going to take a basic math course and also get some tutoring. My math's so bad, I need the tutoring. Every day. (Laughs.) I'm going to do that and then go back to school in the fall, I think.

I've always been a little bit afraid of going to school. I think that's why when I was laid off before, I went back to school to that

Mott Continuing Education, the nursing classes, and got a feel of it.

Because I thought at that point maybe I should go back to school. I didn't think I'd ever go back to General Motors. So I thought, Well, maybe I'll do this.

From there I ended up taking a course that was seventeen weeks long and I went from there to private homes working. That was my first step.

I don't know whatever happened in my life to start saying, No, you can't, you know. I don't know whatever did happen. Because I've always sat back saying, No, Faith, you can't do that, you can't do it. And I don't know why I ever did that. But it was in me to tell myself I couldn't do something.

I just always was like that and just all of a sudden, in the last four or five years, I've just decided that, Yeah, you can. You can do anything you want to do. You've just got to put your mind to it. And go for it.

I think a lot of it is to show my kids the importance of school. You know, what it is to get a job. That's one thing.

I guess at one point, I thought, Oh, they'll get a job. But I can't stress to them enough now what it is to get a job and it's going to be a lot harder in the future.

And I guess in a way, I'm trying to show them what I can do and that they can do it, too. I think you have to set examples for your kids. If you have college in mind, I think your kids will have a tendency to follow that. They'll say, Hey, Mom's doing it, maybe I should go to school. You know.

So, I think we have to set examples. And I want to go back. I didn't for a long time. I'm still scared about it. But I want to go. And I want to be something. I don't want to depend on somebody. I want to be able to do things myself.

For a change. Instead of saying, Hey, Dad, can you come over and fix this? Or, Dad, can you come over and fix that? I think over the years I've wanted to become more independent.

And I've also had a rough relationship. And I think that's also changed me, too. I'm not married, just with a friend. But it's been a rough relationship and I think that's had a lot to do with it.

I think I was always the doting person who said, Okay, okay, whatever. And for some reason, something hit me, you know, of like . . . it was like overnight. I said I'm tired of this.

I've just kind of drawn that line and said, Hey, I want to be somebody. I want to do something with my life. I want to go somewhere. I want to have things.

Through that relationship of always waiting on a guy, you know. I don't want to do that anymore. I want to do it myself.

I never felt safe with General Motors. Paper talk, too [newspaper]. I read the paper a lot and I thought, Gee, you know. It doesn't look good. And I guess I always had that in the back of my mind.

From first layoff I figured: They laid me off once. They could lay me off again.

I've never felt that I'd always get called back.

I'm not really sure what changed me.

I've been through some of the roughest times. Where I didn't have a penny in my pocket. Maybe all the changes all together, a combination of them all.

But I think a lot of it was just working for General Motors and getting laid off and then going back again. I decided this time, I don't want to go back. I just . . . It's not secure.

And I want something that's secure for me. I don't want to be back at General Motors and then back out on the street again. I don't want a life like that. You can take electricity anywhere. I don't care to go anywhere else right now, but I could.

I'd like to stay right at Ron's, watch his empire grow. And I really think it's going to. It's exciting.

I was born in Grand Rapids and then we moved here and my father's always been a GM employee, a superintendent downtown. We've all worked at General Motors and I've seen people come and go and listened a lot, you know, to the talk of my father's friends over at the house.

I've listened to them say, well, General Motors is going to be bad. And I guess I've always picked up on that.

But you never know on jobs with General Motors. Times might be rough now. Seems like it goes in periods. It's good for a while and then it gets rough and it's good for a while and then it gets rough.

You have people say, Oh, it's going to open back up. You don't know, it might. It might not. But I don't want to wait around to see if it does or it doesn't.

Everybody's got to hope. And there's nothing wrong with hoping. When they start talking about closing plants, I think people ought to start thinking about it, you know. Seriously.

I was never angry and I didn't ever really feel that General Motors owed me anything. I've just looked at it as a job. A means of support for my family.

And, angry? No. It's a business, just like any other business.

They start losing money, they've got to cut back. And they still are, still losing money. And when they start losing money, what else can they do but lay people off? They can't pay them if they don't have the money.

I didn't get a lot of help from the union. I was in 659 before. I never really dealt with the union. I never had to.

I had a variety of things I did. I had hurt myself in the shop and I ended up having surgery done. So they stuck me in—they called it the "cripple crib" and I had to work from there and I drove trucks and I tested brakes and I built panels for the sides of trucks. I laid carpet. I swept floors. I built the engines for a while. I did all the wiring. I put the fans on.

I was never on one job for very long. Then I went on inspection. I just kind of shifted around. I wanted to go into welding because I figured, Gee, General Motors is laying off people; I'm going to get laid off.

Tried to get into welding, because then you're learning something and you can use that outside. But I couldn't get into it. So I said, Well, I guess I have to stay pushing the broom or doing inspection at that point. That's what I was doing when I left. And it was a pretty good job but it wasn't for me. I like a job where I'm busy.

Now . . . I get frustrated with General Motors for the things that people were doing down there. Maybe because I'm from a supervisor's background, you know, my family. But I see these people that are sitting around, reading newspapers, not doing their jobs, leaving the plants. That's why we don't have jobs.

And I can understand . . . I don't think it's General Motors' fault. You can kind of look at it from both sides. They just take advantage of General Motors. I mean, people are walking out with stuff, even foremen are walking out with stuff.

I didn't like that 'cause people didn't pull their weight. I didn't like that. And I didn't like seeing people walking out of the plants so freely. Getting paid for not working. I was there, working eight, nine, ten, eleven and a half hours a day. They should have been, too.

I was getting paid for doing a job. Not for taking off and going to the bar or going wherever else. I didn't think that was right.

I think that people at General Motors they always . . . well, when people were getting laid off, they brought people up from Line One up to Line Two.

Well, these people got on these jobs and I believe they had like fifty-six, sixty some jobs an hour on Line One. Then on Line Two it was half that. But the difference was, on Line One, you had less work. Because you had more trucks coming through. So you had less work on your job. Where you went up to Line Two you had less trucks, but you had more work.

Those people were writing up these jobs to where they feel they have too much to do on their job. And then they complained to a committeeman to see if they can't get their job cut down. It wasn't any different, it was just that there were less trucks. But they didn't want to work it that way. They didn't want to have that much on their job. They wanted less work. Yeah, yeah, it was really strange.

I liked the fact that we had the benefits. And the paid vacations. All of that was really great. But I was never angry at General Motors and I was angry at some of the people that took advantage of General Motors. That did frustrate me.

I have this friend of mine on skilled trades. I see them all the time. They do a job. They get the rest of the night to sit and play cards. They get paid $16 an hour if not more. And that's all they do, is play cards all night. Boy, who wouldn't like to make that money? But to me, it's boring to have to sit in a shop all night and read a magazine.

I don't understand that. I think that when they've got a job, I guess they could work not as many down there. Because they have so many that they're just sitting around, half of them. And some nights they don't even have a job to do. I realize that they need them, but I just have to wonder if they don't have an overabundance right now.

So, it's no wonder that General Motors is closing these plants. And the quality on them is not . . . I can remember working on inspection. This tail light on the Suburbans is out. Go to the other side of the truck and it was just as square as could be. And I pointed this out. And I said, "Hey, this needs to be fixed."

"Oh," the foreman said, "we've tried, we've talked to people, we've tried moving it and nothing's been done with it." I said, "Well, you can't ship it like that." I said, "I'm chalking it up."

So I would write it up and say I didn't approve of it. It would go down the line and this other guy would say, Ah, let it slide. You know. So I would keep writing them up. Finally I had the supervisor over there and the general foreman. And they're all saying, "What are you writing these up for?"

I said, "Well, look at them. They're not right. You guys are shipping these." I said I wouldn't ship them.

"Oh, it's just something minor." Well, if they look at that little thing like that and let it go, why not let everything else go down the line?

You know. Quality, they want quality. They don't have quality. Even the supervisors do not enforce it down there. They're in a rush to get everything out. They want to meet their quota. They want to beat first shift in getting out more trucks. But I just feel that the quality is more important if they want to sell these trucks.

It's really strange how they let stuff go. Finally, they started bringing people in. And they were drawing up new plans and they were trying to get it to where they fit it in there. But it took me two months to get them to fix it. Or at least trying to. And when I left, I was still writing them up.

But the guy that's on the job now, he said, "Ah, I've just given up." I said, "Don't give up." I said, "That's poor quality. Don't give up. Keep fighting and eventually, they will straighten it." I said, "They will in time, Just keep pushing it."

Even today I was trying to do this panel with the wire and it's a small panel. Of course, I'm not really good at wiring yet, and you have to get your fingers in there between these wires and number them and keep them straight.

And you want to get them squared off. And trying to get those wires to go square—ha! I was ready to spit tacks today. And Ron does like it neat. 'Course I do, too.

And I'm trying to get it to where it looks neat and the wires—I'm trying to get them to go the way I want them to. By the time I finished there, I was so frustrated with those wires and myself because I felt that I could have done better on it.

I ride on myself pretty heavy when it comes to perfection. I notice that even at home I'm the same way. You know, if there's a spot on the carpet, you know, it's got to be picked up. Things have got to be in a certain order.

And there's a lot of pride in your work. It is a sense of accomplishment when you're done. Even today I surprised myself. I had help with Gloria. But it was the first time I had ever done the button.

I'd look at the print and I'd go back and say, "Now, Gloria, is this the way I'm to do it?" And I'd have her look at it so it wasn't wired wrong.

And she said, "Yeah." And I felt good inside. I thought, Hey, I did it. I figured it out first and then I went to her and made sure on it. And it really was kind of neat. The feeling inside that I had that I had accomplished it.

Because this is something that you built yourself. And it is—it's exciting when it's all done. It's yours and nobody else has done anything to it. It's kind of a neat feeling when you're done with it all.

You want to know what's funny? Before I was laid off, I was sitting at work and I thought, What am I going to do after I get laid off? And I thought, Well, gee, if I want to be an electrician—and this is what was strange—maybe I'll be a small parts electrician, electronics. And I thought maybe I'd go into that.

There's good money in that. Especially when you're talking about these VCR's, the cam corders, there's good money in that if you're good at what you're doing. And I thought, Boy, that'd be a good way to make good money. Get a little business going of your own and . . . I thought maybe I'd go into that. And then when this electricity or working doing the panels and stuff, I thought, Hey, that sounds better.

I can't really explain what made me decide to go. It was the skill. I think I would have to say it's the skill of learning something instead of just going out and driving a truck. Anybody can drive a truck. Anybody can. This is using your brain, you know.

And I guess I was always lazy with my brain. All of a sudden I wanted to start using it. So. It was really weird, though, I was talking about electronics. And then this came along. Here I'd thought about it and talked about it. And thought about going back to school. On the other hand I said, No, no, I can't go back to school.

This gives me more of a feeling on-the-job training. I've got the TAPP funds to go back to school. I've got all the opportunities right now in front of me.

Sometimes that's what I need—a push—and working with Ron is excellent because he's a pusher. He doesn't stand there and show you. He says, Hey, come on, do it. Whether you're unsure of yourself or not. He doesn't care. You're going to do it.

Yeah, it's hands-on. It sure is. It's kind of different. I guess I'm the kind of person who needs that little bit, you know, more so than others. And even I need a push at going to school. But this time I'm pushing myself.

I think school will be a lot easier with on-the-job training. I don't know what I have to take when I go back. I don't know if I have to take the basics in college. I want to skip all that stuff, you know, and go to the electronics. The blueprint reading, you know, the math that I need. Science wouldn't be bad either because they's so much in science that you can use.

There's going to be a lot to learn and I'm still scared and I've still got to hit myself and say, Hey, you've got that opportunity. You're lucky.

I feel that I am lucky to have the opportunity to have a job like this, get the hands-on training and also go to school.

When I'd get home from going in the shop, I was just going to work, just the same old repetitious stuff. I'd be on cripple cage and I could go on any job. But it's still, once you got the job down, you knew it was the same thing every day.

Here, it's not. Every day is different down here. Not one day's the same. And I go into work and I've got this feeling. It's like I'm ready to explode. It's excitement. It's like a high that I've gotten.

It's just the excitement of going in and learning something and what I was going to do that day. It's also just learning things, using my brain again.

I think what I'd have to tell someone else who is laid off, is don't sit and think that GM's going to call you back. Look ahead and make plans for something else.

If they want to go back to General Motors and they call them back, then go back to General Motors. But in the meantime, don't sit back and do nothing. Take advantage of what is offered to you now. Go to school. Go see the HRC programs. The training. Anything you can to better yourself.

I'm less afraid, now that I've started. But not a great deal. (Laughs.) I go in nervous every day and the big thing is my measuring and I'm scared to death I might put a hole off-center. You do that and you've got a ruined door there, and what else can you do with it? It has to be in a certain spot. I've never had to do it by myself yet and soddering and trying to figure out the print and stuff like that. I get scared still.

There's something inside that gets me scared.

I don't know what a lot of people are going to do without General Motors. But I know I'm not going to be one of them that sits back and does nothing And hopes that they call me back. And I doubt if I'll ever go back, but anybody that has been laid off through General Motors, I think they ought to go out, start looking for a job. Find something. Learn a skill. Something that they can take anywhere.

Go to school.

I've always felt that a job like this [electrician] is something in my line because I've always liked being busy. With my hands. And even to this day if I'm not smoking a cigarette or drinking a cup of coffee I'm always doing something. And this kind of job here I'm always doing something.

And it sounds like me. It really does. Even now, I'm having a hard time holding my fingers still, you know, I just really . . .

I took those aptitude tests the first time so I didn't have to do it again. And I knew where I needed the help in. And at that time I just didn't want to get it. I found out that I was good with my hands in building stuff, things like that. So that fits in with it.

Sometimes you've got to bite the bullet. And I guess, as they say, you've got to take chances. I mean, there's risks in anything you do. And you can't always have everything you want.

And I figure that with me I've just got to have patience. You know, my friend is always saying to me, Faith, go find another job. He says find another job where you're going to make more money. Where you're going to have a regular forty hours right now.

And I tell myself, No. I don't want to. All's I've got to do is have patience. And stick with it.

Because I know it's going to be rough now, but look at down the line what's going to happen. And that's what I've got to look at. People go through rough times. Heck, I've been through a lot of rough times. You know. So what's a few more rough times temporarily?

Because I know down the line it's going to be a lot better.

I worry now. I worry now about money. Because I'm not making the kind of money like what I did. But I got to say, Hey, times are tough but we've got to make due with them. And I just look at down the road, what it's going to be like down there and just bite the bullet now and go after it.

That's all I can do.

You know, there's something I have to say. I guess I used to be a negative person. I can remember my mother always saying to me, Faith, you can't do that. Faith, you can't do that. So over a period of time that kind of went into my head.

And then I have been with a really negative man for the last several years. But do you know, that's helped. It has. It has because through him I have become a more positive person. You get tired of it. You get tired of somebody being so negative. And then you start being positive.

I probably used to be a negative person. You know, at one point. But through him and being with him I've become a more positive person.

What I see is that I don't like what he does, sees things so negative and I think, Boy, am I like that? I hope not. If I am, I want to change that part of me.

I'm going after it. I've got dreams and plans and just the only way I can get them is if I go after this.

I get scared of failing at times. I mean on this job. You know, I go and set myself up here and I'm . . . I have this fear of not doing it right. That scares me, you know, it really does.

But you know, it's going to happen, it's really going to happen. People are going to lose benefits, they're not going to be able to find a job. And that gets depressing when you can't find a job. And people are . . . They even say that at times like this is when people start committing suicide and all these strange things. Crime. You know, hey.

But I won't let myself get to that point. I mean there's always a chance that something might happen where I might not have a job. I can do anything if I put my mind to it.

People, they need to have patience. You know, don't let yourself get frustrated because there are jobs out here. People are looking for jobs that pay the same wages as General Motors. They're not going to find them. You know. There might be a few, here and there. You might hit one. But they're not going to find what they had.

They're going to have to lower their expectations.

But I wasn't moving. Nope. My family's here. I guess if I was married or something and my husband wanted to move, I'd move. I really wouldn't want to because my family's here.

As a single parent, I don't want to move. I think of myself going to some other state or something and seeing people I don't know, you know, the area I don't know. The stores, you don't know where to shop. Not knowing anybody. Just the support, you don't have it. If you go with a group of people, it'd be all right. From one area.

But I just don't have that behind me that I could do that. I don't have to.

Do you know, I would like to have a home. I've always had apartments or where I've lived with someone. I did have a trailer. That's something I'd like to do is have a home and an education and security. I guess it's something I haven't really had in a while. Something secure.

A combination of everything, having the job, having the education within the next five years, being more than what I am now. Down the road there will be a lot more money with what I'm doing now.

I don't know, I've wrote that question down five years ago. (Laughs.) In the meantime, I've sold my trailer and moved in with a guy and my goals are never reached. (Laughs.)

There's always changes and we just have to make adjustments as the changes come. And I guess I've never been one to . . .

Over the years I've learned to say, Okay, this is what it's going to be like, make the adjustment. What can you do to change it?

There's always changes and you've got to learn to make the adjustments with the changes and you can't sit and worry about them. I mean, you can't, you're wasting too much time. You really are.

And what does it give you? It gives you headaches. It gives you low self-esteem. It just . . . it tears you up. I haven't got time to get down here again. I want to get up here. So if I sit here and worry about it I'm not going to go anywhere. So I just go with the flow.

You asked me what I could tell somebody else from General Motors. I would definitely have to say, "Be patient." And it's not going to come all at once. And you've just got to be patient and have faith that you're going to find something. And have some confidence in yourself and just go for whatever you can. You've got the opportunity to go to school, do something with it. Use that education. Become more of what you are.

Well, I'm going to have to pay for education, you know, part of it, because I've only got so much time. I'll have to pay for a lot of it but I figure that in the long run, it's going to be worth it.

Four years or five years or whatever it is to go to school to get my journeyman. What is that? In four years, I'll have it easy. You know, you've got to struggle.

If I don't struggle now, I'm going to have to struggle even harder in five years if I don't go to school. So why not struggle now? Take that chance and do it now.

But you know what's so hard for people who go to school, a lot of times? You go out and you find these jobs and the guy says during the interview, "Well, what kind of experience do you have?" You know.

Now I was lucky, I really am lucky in all ways because I've got the experience and the training.

I feel lucky. Because there's a lot of people out there that don't have jobs. And do you know, since that article came out in the paper [a *Flint Journal* article about her boss hiring laid-off workers], we have had umpteen million calls. People dropping in resumes, you know.

And if I hadn't had that at that time, you know, made that decision, I would be one of the people calling. That's right. So in a sense, I feel lucky. I really do.

I like Ron, he's excellent. You couldn't ask for a better boss.

I think he will talk to you about anything. He's excellent. He is. He took us out to lunch today. How many bosses do that?

He certainly does know his business and he was a dropout. He was a high school dropout. And he said, he was talking today about going back to school and his math. He said, "I didn't know two plus two. But when I went back to college," he said, "I sat down and spent twenty hours on one problem, but I was going to get it."

Hey, if he can do it, I can do it, too. It's just all right here. [Points to her head.] It's up to you. You've got to make a decision within yourself and say, "I'm going to do it."

I've even noticed that at home sometimes, now, I sit and I'll look at the electrical work and I'll look around and I think, Someday, I'm going to be able to do this. That's exciting. It really is.

12

Burns

*Gloria Burns had worked for General Motors for nine years, trans-
ferring to the Lake Orion plant, then returning to Flint for a final
layoff. Like Faith Ellis, she is learning how to be an electrician.
Their boss, Ron Panter, owns an electrical paneling business but
still works for General Motors as a journeyman electrician.*

*Although Ellis was hired through the help of the HRC,
Burns had already agreed to work without wages just for the
experience of learning a new skill.*

*Burns is a petite brunette in her early forties, with a light,
wispy voice. She has been divorced once and is now remarried.*

I'm not at a point where I can go back to school right now; I
need some money. So I went looking for work. Then Ron said he'd
try to train me. So I thought, Well, while I'm getting my benefits
I'm going to try to pick up anything I can, you know.

Ron said, "I'm going to give you a chance." At first, he didn't
pay me because he didn't have any money to pay me. But he gave
me a chance to learn something.

From the very beginning, it wasn't like Ron didn't want to
pay me. He said, "I don't have it right now." He wasn't taking
advantage of me. He was just starting out his business. It was he
didn't have it. He was trying to get where he is in the business.

I thought, Well, if he needs somebody and I definitely need
some skills, what can I stand to lose?

When I first started I said, "I'm not a girl, you know. Don't be
thinking of me as a girl because I'm not one of the girls." And Ron
doesn't look at you like that. I mean, I don't like to use the excuse
I'm a woman. I can't do this and I can't do that.

I said, "But Ron, if I tried something and I try and I tell you I
can't, then I can't." And he understands that. He said, "Yup, no

157

place in this place for girls." He said, "We have no girls, no women around here. We have electricians."

See, I was there working for Ron at less wages. Okay? And HRC come out with wanting to bring Faith in there or this other girl who was one of the two they were going to send and see which one was better suited for the job.

So I asked them, I was talking to Dave Rhodes. And Ron said, "Well, she's laid off from GM, too." And they said, "You are? Are you within our program?" And I said, "No, you sent me some information, but I have been through the orientation and the battery of tests you gave before and they didn't do anything for me. They just said go back to school."

So he said to me, "Well, maybe we can help you, too, to get more training." They've got a contract to pay part of my wages for three months and Faith's for six months.

Right. With the understanding that at the end of the time Ron will keep us and he will increase our wages. Because we're helping his business and he's getting some assistance in our wages.

Well, Dave Rhodes told me, "I don't know if [I] can help [you] or not because you're already here." And I said, "Wait a minute, I'm in the same situation. The only thing is . . ." He said, "Yeah, but you're working." And I said, "Yeah, I went to work instead of staying out of work. I was trying to pick up skills on my own."

I told him, "What you're telling me is that I'm going to be penalized because I offered to work for free, trying to pick up my own skills because I didn't think anybody was going to hire me and I don't want to be at McDonald's working. Okay? Or Taco Bell. I want something that I can sell for a lot more money down the road."

And he said, "Well, I didn't say I can't help you. I don't know. Let me go check." And he went back and he talked to them and he said, Sure.

It's also stipulated [at HRC] that if you were making less money at your new job than what you made at General Motors, you still were eligible. And see that's where they got me in. So that's where they helped me. I'm still not making General Motors wages. But it's higher than I would get anyplace else.

The first time I looked at a wiring panel I was scared. I said, "Ron, that's just like me giving you a bridal gown pattern and material and a sewing machine and saying go to it. I don't understand this." So he said, "That's right." And he explained to me, slower, "This wire goes here and then here," and so on. So I could get it.

You know, it scares me to think that even at this, I'm learning but I'm still not at the point where I could go somewhere else. But it's still scary because I've got a lot of things to learn here. And I think you're always scared to take on something new, wondering if you're capable of accomplishing it.

Even now after a whole year. I mean this is just one phase of it and there's so many things you need to know.

But Ron knows so much. He is so smart. Like he says, "I'm a high school dropout. And you can do it if you want to, you can." I mean, he's really smart.

And I think, Well, as long as he keeps pouring information out of his mouth, some of it's got to sink into my head. And I'll keep asking him, you know.

A lot of times he'll tell me something and then I'll ask him about it again and he'll tell me and I'll say, "Oh, I knew that."

He'll say, "Yeah, you did know that." (Laughs.)

But he doesn't get upset that I don't remember.

There's been other things that came up and he'll be explaining it to me and he says, "Well, you're going to know more about that when you get into school because you'll be learning that." I think the book learning with the hands-on training will help.

To just sit and look at a book and try to comprehend everything I need to know, I don't think that would be easy for me. But maybe the combination of on-the-job training and the books will be good.

But the whole thing is really interesting. I just don't have anything else that I would want to be doing right now. I mean not even to go back to General Motors. And I know I'd make more money there. Right now.

But I feel like, Hey, if I can stick with this, there's a lot of money to be made. I've seen.

He [boss Ron Panter] wants to get out of General Motors so he's trying to get this business going, and make it profitable. I told him, "I know if you make it then I'm going to make it. And if I work hard enough so that I know what I'm doing you're not getting rid of me." He wants to get into this full-time. And right now he works like twenty hours a day between GM and here.

He's an electrician in there. GM electrician. Well, he wants to go on his own. Because there's a lot of money to be made in this field. Especially building the electrical panels, getting out of the residential and commercial wiring and getting into building some of these panels.

He designs them and he does the drawings for them. And there's a lot of money on the outside.

We're building stuff for GM but outside bids are put out on the market, put out in the field. And we get them through like Advance Electric and different wholesale houses. I mean, they're picking them up, okay? We need such and such to be built. All these changes are being made to update these factories, you know? Every day there's something new that comes on in the electrical field.

I just don't see where there's going to be totally no work at all. There may be days when it's slower than other days, but I just think Ron wants this business too bad. He's just tied up too much time and money in it to let it go down the drain. He's such a hard, ambitious person.

And if he stays driven, then we're going to have a job and as long as I stay driven, then I can be something that can be profitable for him.

You know, a lot of people said, "Well, what happens later down the road if he says, 'I don't need you.'" I said, "He won't do that 'cause he's just not that kind of a person. He gave me a chance when I didn't know anything, so if I'm a benefit to him then he's not going to get rid of me for somebody else." I just know.

I think it's because I worked at GM, a sure thing, and then they think, Well, what else have you done but work at GM? And after you're on a job a few days there anybody can do it. It's just most of the time repetition. The hourly is same thing, you know, nothing changes.

You do get bored in there. But with this, I haven't had a chance to get bored. Some days I go home aggravated because there was just so much to try to learn or do. But I go back the next day and it becomes a little easier.

After I had been working a while, two months or so ago, I went down to my mom and dad's. And my Dad was putting in new service. This other guy was working with him. He was putting in a new service box in his house, but he was going to rewire it himself. So I told him, "If you need some help, let me know. 'Cause I would love to help you. It's experience and I'd like to help you."

Well, I went down there and my ex-husband was there. And he's sitting at the table. My dad was doing it wrong, okay? And I just asked him, "Dad, why are you doing it this way? You're doing it wrong."

And he said, "What do you mean?" I said, "Well you're supposed to pigtail the code states that come off of the pigtail instead of hooking all the wires in the back of this duplex." The duplex is the plug you plug your appliances into. And he was putting all these wires in the back of this. On the back of your plug is this place to put your wire in, okay? But actually, you're only supposed to come in with two wires, a black wire and a white wire and then a ground wire.

Well, he was bringing in three blacks, three whites. He was bringing them all into this plug instead of pigtailing, which means take an extra piece of wire and just hook it together, twist it, and put a wire net on it. That's called pigtailing.

But he wasn't wanting to pigtail. He was wanting to put all these on wrong and I'm trying to get him to do it my way. Okay? The right way. And he said, "Nope, we're going to do it this way." And I said, "Well, why, Dad? It's just as easy and it doesn't cost any more money and let's do it the correct way."

And my ex-husband sits there, "Yup, yup, yup, she thinks she's an electrician now. She thinks she's an electrician." And he was being smart about it, too.

It's the code, the national code, that states that's the way it has to be done. So I was just trying to explain to him the right way and he just wasn't going to do it my way. You know, he was just being hardheaded.

And then my dad asked me, "Okay, you think you're an electrician, how do you hook up this light?" He had this situation where he had two switches and he wanted to hook up a light in the basement and then one upstairs. But he wanted them to go off individually or come on individually.

I said, "Well, I don't know, let me find out. I'm not quite sure, but I'll find out." So I went to Ron and I asked him, "How would we do this?"

So he explained to me the way we had to do it. And I went back to my dad and he said, "Well, I don't want to do it that way. Like, can't we do it with a white wire coming in instead of a black?" (Laughs.) I said, "Because you're not supposed to." "Who said I can't?" he said. No matter what, my word isn't—you know, not yet—it's not good enough for anything.

I mean, he'll ask me how to do something but when I tell him, then he doesn't want to do it my way.

I don't know, I guess he just doesn't feel . . . He'll ask me how to do something and when I find out and tell him, then he questions me. And I told Ron when I came home that last time, in fact, the next day, I said, "Don't you ever tell me again how to do something for my dad. If I come in and ask you, you tell me how to do it so I know. But you don't let me ever tell him anything again!"

It's just they can't believe that I'm capable of doing this stuff. Ron thinks I am and the businesses that buy the stuff I build are very pleased by them. That's more important to me. Yeah.

I think some people just sit back thinking, Well, this is just something [she's] going to think [she's] going to do and [she'll] never go through with it, so that makes me want to be successful even more.

Anyway, Ron had enough confidence in me. So if he believes I can, I believe with him helping me and my own ambitions that I will do it.

There's a theory behind electricity. And I'll learn all that, I'm sure, when I go to school. The basics. But I believe that the on-the-job training is going to help a great deal.

The way I was before, you know, I could hook up a duplex to wire it, stick it back in the wall. I could do that, but I didn't mess with anything. I mean, there's no schematics I could read, size of the wires. I didn't know that for 30 inch, you had to use a number 10 wire. And still to this day, Faith [co-worker] will say to me, "Well, how do you know to use this size wire?" Well, if it doesn't state it, then I ask Ron. And there's formulas for figuring out what size wire you need for the amps that's produced by whatever motor or whatever. There's ways to find out what to use. You know, I can't run asking Ron all my life.

Yeah, of course, I feel better about myself. Oh, I'm scared on one hand that I'm going to have to learn and get my feet wet. You know, by starting over. But every time I learn something and I get some feedback that, "Hey, that was a good job," that makes me feel real good. And I've got a lot of that through knowing Ron and through the business, the stuff we've sold.

When I first started there, one guy called and I was working on his panel and he wanted to talk to a journeyman, 'cause he wanted to talk to someone who knew something about the panel that he was having done. When he finished it, he told Ron, "Well, that's the nicest looking panel." Ron said, "Gloria did it." He said, "God, that looks better than any we've had." And Ron has even pointed out that my panels look better than the journeyman's. And he said, "And they work, too." So that makes you feel good.

I don't know. My girlfriend and her husband both are laid off and he's got sixteen years in General Motors. He doesn't want them to offer him relocation. He doesn't want to leave this area. But he's not wanting to go to school. I don't know what people like that are going to do.

You have relatives, see, that was like me going to Lake

Orion. I would have stayed there. I would have moved my kids down there, but they didn't want to move. My family was here and they didn't want to move. So. Otherwise I would have been to Pontiac and I would have been down there when the layoff came. And you're starting all over in a new job and everybody's making new friends and new people—I mean, that's scary in itself.

Another friend was laid off. Her and her husband, they're both in school. She's going back to school in, I'm not quite sure, it's through HRC. I think it's cafeteria management or cook training. I haven't talked to her, but I've heard she's going back. And she's in a program, I think, that lasts six months. And her husband's been going to school all along. But he's going to be a CPA. So he's been planning on training. I mean, over the years he has worked on it.

But I just know so many people that aren't doing anything. They're just sitting back and saying, well, we're going to get another extension. They have to give another extension with everybody laid off. They've got to put second shift back on at Buick. You know. Then you hear this rumor that in March they're going to start building the Park Avenue there or another car there. People are hanging onto that.

Well, they're just going to do that, say, Well, I'll get called back. Which, they may, I don't know.

People are wanting to walk into another job that pays thirteen dollars an hour, fourteen dollars an hour with benefits. And you don't walk out of General Motors with the skills that they taught you and get a job at thirteen dollars, fourteen dollars an hour.

And a lot of them don't want to settle for less.

But for everybody to go start their own business, they can't financially. A lot of them don't have the skills to start their own business.

Five years ago, no one would have believed that GM would have shut down these plants the way they have. I mean, when you stop and think. Okay, I was laid off. So. *They're going to call me back. It's just sales are down. Well, they're going to call me back.*

Like I said, my girlfriend's husband has got sixteen years and he's still saying, well, you know. See, I have been laid off, too, before—two and a half years and they called me back.

I think a lot of them were hoping for corporate seniority which meant that they would have flowed into the other plants, you know, and the lower seniority people would have been laid off. I don't know what their ideas are.

I have a brother-in-law that just was laid off at Fisher Body out here. He's a truck driver. He's only staying, I guess, to help clean out the plant. He's got twenty-eight years. He didn't even sign up to go to Buick. Twenty-eight years. And he's got nothing after March.

He's too young to retire. Can't financially afford retirement. That's it. And he had a chance to go to Buick with his seniority and he turned it down, thinking, Fisher Body's going to stay open and I'm going to have a job. He thought he was going to stay at Fisher Body. Fisher 1. He had a chance to go to Buick when Fisher people went to Buick, but he turned that down. I don't understand what some people's thinking was.

It's not going to happen. GM's not going to close this plant. And I think that's what the idea was and if they would have offered training and said, "Okay, we're closing," some—small, not the majority—would have taken advantage of it.

They were all waiting on this false hope that another car was going to be brought in there.

But you know, I think if they would have offered some of these guys with twenty years seniority or sixteen years training earlier . . . okay, 'cause these same guys that were in there could have taken advantage of the funds and went back to school and could have been working on an education so they'd have something to fall back on.

You're talking four years. A lot of them could have been working [toward a degree]. And they didn't. And now they're saying, Okay, we've got six months benefits 'cause unemployment runs out in six months. The SUB-fund is lower they're taking more than one credit now, so your SUB-credits. Like I had fifty-two; they didn't last a year. They started taking more than one and then it got up to two and a quarter the last one I drew, and I know it's higher than that now.

So some of these people now won't even last six months. And when I got laid off, my SUB lasted longer. There were less people laid off. But the more people goes out, the quicker you use your SUB-credits. So they're not even going to have benefits as long as I did. And they're sitting there waiting for this extension, which the extension may come in, but . . .

And even at that, it doesn't mean that you're going to have a job and it doesn't mean that you're going to have money in a year. Because how long is the state going to just keep giving extensions to people?

But when you think most of these people in GM—I don't know if it's the majority—but a lot of them have never gone to school. Like me. They walked out of high school and either got married or started having kids, got a job right out of high school and so they have no skills. And the idea of going back to school is really scary to me.

Just recently I took some computer courses that were at Buick. But I didn't go into the college classes with professors. I'm sure it wasn't like college professors. The teachers at OE Learning [company hired to do training inside the plant] are different because they're a smaller business which GM and the UAW they brought in there. So they were a smaller environment. Like, Call me, here's my phone number, call me if you need me, call me at home.

And my brother-in-law, he went to Mott and it was like, he was begging for information and couldn't get anyone to help him.

And see, I haven't been in a classroom situation in a long time. But I know I can do it because Ron will help me and Shelley [daughter] she can help me. She's really good in school.

They will. I know they will. I don't have to feel like I'm going to fall back on them, but if I need them they're there.

It's scary when you're on your own. If I thought I had to go back to school and I didn't have Ron there to help me and think, Okay, can I do this? Am I going to be able to keep up my school work at night and am I going to be able to work here in the daytime?

We're working about seven hours a day right now. Seven straight hours and so there's no time then for school work. At work. So it's at night.

But I do feel like if there was a problem I could take it in there and say, Ron, I don't understand this. And he'd be able to help me.

I'm the kind of person that needs that extra little push. I mean it's something interesting, you like it, but you need somebody to say, Okay.

Like someone I know right now, neither one of them, her and her husband, are worried about getting back into retraining. Well, their idea is, We'll just file for bankruptcy. I mean, when you're used to living on two General Motors checks and then suddenly . . . you know. You're still not—they're not going to have any money coming in. They're not going to have any unemployment left. They're not going to have any SUB left.

And you went from living on sixty, seventy thousand dollars a year and so bankruptcy, and you're still not going to have any money coming in. That's still going to mess your mind.

And I feel so much better. Even when I first started working for nothing because I was trying to build my skills. And I was learning things.

See, I'm not a cryer. Well, some things I've went home and cried after I got home because it's been a rough day. But no one is terrible to me. You know, if I had had to work with people who expected me to know the job right off and were really hard to get along with and stuff, that would be . . . I'd probably cry at home a lot more. But that just doesn't happen.

Ron is great, he just really is. I don't know why he ever took a chance on me. In General Motors, he didn't see me do that much. I didn't have any skills there. I was there every day, so maybe that showed him that I would come to work.

He already told me he'd bid for a job to go into Buick. He bid through another company. They had put this job out for bid. It was like ten different places bidding on it. And we bid on it. But he already told them that if he goes in there, he's hiring laid-off GM employees to go in and do that. He said, "Every one of them will be electricians. But I'm going to hire the guys you laid off to take back in there with me."

He said, "But the difference is they'll be working for me. But you're going to pay GM scale."

So, I mean, he's not out to get the union and he's not out to beat GM. But he's out to do a good job. And I know he does a good job in GM, plus he wants a good job done in his shop. And he expects that out of us.

And he is smart. And he understands that we don't know everything that you need to know. But he also sits back and he knows who actually wants to work and who is just kind of riding along.

I don't like working with somebody if you're putting forth everything that you possibly can. And when you tell me you can't, then, well, you can't.

If I sat down and cried he'd probably listen for a minute or two, but he just doesn't sit back and say, Well, you can't do that because you're a woman. No.

I keep telling him I don't want to work with women. Don't put me in here with a bunch of women because women say, *I can't do this. I can't do that.* Are we going to sit around here and drink coffee and visit? I don't like that situation. I want to work, do what I have to do and get out of here. And I want to get it done the best I can.

So that's the way we've always worked. And he gets along fine with that because he wants a good quality job and he's not rushing you, but he wants it done as quick as you can get it done. And if I come to him and say, All right, I need tomorrow off, I need to take off two hours early. Well, then he has no problem with that.

'Cause see, I like that kind of a situation.

And that's another advantage of working for him. Because he feels the same way I do about working, where if you get in a big situation with GM it's: *We're just here to do what we have to do and when our eight hours are up we want to go home.*

I went in there at night on a Saturday night and have done work. Well, I had to go to a funeral and I said, "Ron, can I take off?" He said sure. He didn't say anything to me, but I could see, like, Well, you got to get that job done by Monday. And I said, "Your job will be done Monday. This job here will be done Monday."

And he said, "Sure, no problem."

So I mean, I'm in there at ten o'clock a Saturday night wiring a panel, you know? But my husband come with me and I'm sitting there and I'm wiring and my husband said, "What can I help you with?" "Just be here with me, because it's dark outside and I'm here all by myself."

I feel we've got a very good boss.

Well, see, every one of our jobs is like a project. It's something that you start it and you have so many days and . . . There's not usually a time limit. Like this one we're working on right now. The guy wants it by Friday. Well, he'll be lucky if he gets it by Friday because he just brought some more stuff in today. But when we actually see what we have to work with, then it's an amount of work until I'm done and I'm so glad when every one of them goes out the door.

It makes you feel real good to know when you're done that you have done something and it's yours. Compared to being in General Motors where you're putting a piece or two on a car and you're seeing it go down the road. So. It's just another car that thirty-five hundred of us built.

I was real lucky, but I do believe that if people just set and wait to get lucky, that's not going to happen to very many of them. Many are waiting to get lucky.

13
Daniel

Remon Daniel works as a mechanic for Massey Inc., a car dealer in Grand Blanc. He is Israeli and had worked for General Motors for six years before he was laid off. Daniel is strikingly good looking—light blue eyes, dark brown hair, a contagious smile—but he looks tired.

I worked for six years. I started in Plant 31, which used to be the gear and axle plant. I got laid off from Buick City. I got transferred so many times. I got laid off November 15; that's when they laid off five thousand people. The first big one.

I was stunned at first. The problem is that when you get laid off from the shop, you know outside of it they don't pay as much. Okay, that's the first thing. Every other place, they won't pay as much as the shop.

So the standard of living comes down right there. I was thinking that they might call me back. But now, knowing that they keep laying off people and closing plants, it's—this time is maybe for good.

Well, I got into what I'm doing now by—I used to work as a mechanic before I came into the country. I used to work for Hank Graff Chevrolet as a mechanic here. And then Buick called me, so I quit my job and I went to work. I worked for three months and I got laid off.

But I had a good job and what happened is that I lost a good job. Which I thought it would be more lasting but it wasn't. I got laid off and I went back to Hank Graff to get a job and they had hired somebody else in my place.

So, I went to the Human Resource Center and I showed my credentials to Dave Rhodes. He's a very nice person. And he picked up the telephone and started making calls. And from the first time I went to see him, I started going out to places for job interviews. Yes.

And then he asked me, "Would you like to work for Massey?" I said yes. He knows Terry personally and he called him and he said, "Yeah, send him over." So I came in and I got the job.

There's a change. I used to work with Chevrolets and now Fords, but I'm adjusting. It's not a problem. I like it here. I'm happy with the job. It's very nice. And the people are good.

I also got, while I was laid off, I went and got a class two license for driving a big truck. I also have that license now. Just in case something to lean on in case I need to. Yeah.

What I was planning to do is try to get a degree. I was planning to get into engineering on a part-time basis. It's not that easy for me now becuase I have two kids. And there is the education and you have to work and then go to school at night. It's kind of tough.

I'm trying to make it work for me to do it. One class at a time.

It is difficult. It takes more effort to get through. I am married. But I'm saying it's easier if you're single with no children.

Having the training is important. You cannot, these days, get a job outside of the shop without some kind of education or knowledge of some kind. Because when you go to an employer to present yourself, you have to have some credentials to show—that's what I've done. Not having it, without credentials, getting a job is not easy; it's very difficult.

I still qualify for TAPP. That's what I've been planning at Mott Adult Education, to use this TAPP money toward an engineering degree.

I like mechanics, I always liked mechanics. Since I was a kid, I've liked mechanics, yes. It is interesting, yes.

But, as I say, what I'd like to get into more is taking more the engineering part, design. It is the same.

Because I was laid off before, okay, you kind of get used to it. I've been out more than once, okay? So, it's kind of like when you get beaten with a hammer on your head. After a while you get used to it, you know? The first time it's painful, but then the second time, you know, it's less and then you get used to it.

I heard just rumors, but I was kind of shocked when . . . because they came around there and they took your badge and they took everything. And that's it. Yeah. And that's the first time. Like someone's in the army and they take their stripes off. (Laughs.)

When they did that, that's when—that night, it was November 14th, because I worked second shift in Buick City on the line.

169

When they did that, I felt that this time it was going to be something serious. For good. Because they took the badge. Always before they never did.

And then they give you a package of paperwork and that's it. That's all that you get. The foreman came around, shook everybody's hand, "Nice knowing you," and that's it. And I haven't been in there since November.

Well, the best thing is always to plan for things ahead of time. First, you have to have a goal of what you're going to do. Okay. And then to plan to open the road for that goal. To make it easier while you're going through it. So you won't get shocked right at once.

When all your benefits run out—I waited, actually, for all my benefits to run out because I had to use them for insurance purposes, you know. And also for, you know, hoping that things would change. But when things got close enough to where I ran out two or three weeks ahead of time, I stopped at HRC, went to Dave Rhodes and you know, started putting in applications.

I had also started looking for work, even before I went to Dave Rhodes. I went as far as Pontiac and as far as Detroit. I found jobs up there but I didn't want to drive that far, you know, every day. It is too far.

And then the same day that I got hired here, I received a call also from a trucking company to work for them for $10 an hour in Detroit. But I turned it down because it's closer to my house here. So I take this job.

Okay, the only thing that changed, actually, is the pay. And that's what counts. (Laughs.) The pay changed, okay? And that's the main thing, actually, that is hard to get used to. Yes, you have a family to support and then your income just starts coming down, you know. You have to pinch, pinch, pinch.

You see, now I make half of what I used to make before. So it is a lot for me. Also, what's important, I did not purchase new things at the time when the rumors started. I did not purchase, like, a new car. I did not have payments. So, I planned. I was aware. If anything happens, I better not have payment schedules to pay.

Some people, you know, if you go buy and then there is no income, you're in trouble. So I did not do that. I would conserve, conserve. And now, you know, I'd like to come back and make more money, but there isn't the same job. So I try to get more education and slowly work myself up, you know. And more seniority here, you know, I will make more money as another place. So I thought it out.

I enjoy what I do. It is interesting. And what's good about it here, also, is that they send me to school to learn. A program. Like, two months ago they sent me to a school to learn about the air bag that comes out of the steering wheel. They sent me to learn about how to diagnose it if there's problems, what to do. And it's interesting.

At the dealership, there's lots of advantages over any other place to work. It's larger and they send you to learn. The small garages they won't, you know. They send you to schools, but not as good as the ones that the manufacturers do.

Well, okay, if you can, get an education. Spend the time to go learn and get a degree. That's the number one thing—that's what to do. Because that's something that you get and nobody can take it away from you. You have it. When you get it, that's it, it's yours.

You have a better chance to find a job with a degree than being just a worker. There is always going to be workers, you know, always. But the people with education, I think it's easier for them to find a job. Anybody can be a worker. There's always lots of workers. But a person with a degree can more easily move around all over the country, than to be just pinned down in one place because you have to follow the factory.

I'm from Israel, I was born in Nazareth. I guess you see us once in a while in the news. That's the Holy Land, you know. It is a beautiful country. I came here in 1976. My family is in Arizona. We came all together. My dad, my mom. I have a brother, also, who works for Buick. We got hired one day apart. He got laid off also.

He got more time than me. I got laid off and stayed out. I was out more. So he got ten years in. My sister lives in Flint, so we decided to go where we had relatives. I think it was a mistake, now, coming to Flint. (Laughs.)

My experience in the shop, as a working place, it's not the best place to work in. I think we got into this situation that is . . . the pay got so high and so soon, every year, every time they had the contract. The wages were so good, but then things are coming around. They are saying these employees are overpaid; they learn to run machines and that's it. They don't have any other training. And things are going backward now. They are paying for all the time that passed. Which I wish that if the factory workers didn't get paid that much in the first place, they would be surviving now and everybody's not laid off.

But the wages jumped so high that it competed with everybody else and now they are complaining to cut down so now they laid off everybody.

I did, myself, turn down overtime. The conditions were bad.

It was Department 1242. It was bad. We were working seven days a week, twelve hours a day. You don't see that very often. Come to work in the dark, go home in the dark. And that's it. And it's too much. So what they should have done is work eight hours and for the overtime, hire somebody else. It's good for some, but why not share it with others, with the ones that are not having a job?

14

Denter

Sandra K. Denter, a robust woman in her late forties, had the unfortunate opportunity to compare how two different plants closed down. She not only worked for General Motors in their Truck and Bus plant in Flint, she had also spent thirteen years as a plant employee for Smeltzer Corporation in Durand.

She begins by describing what her first closing experience was like at the Smeltzer plant.

We had General Motors union, Local 1026, [at Smeltzer's] that we had there and when we went to ratify we were not going out on strike we were just going back to work. They had a few things as far as wording is what we wanted changed in the contract and they locked us out. That was on a Saturday and we went Monday into work, handed in our badges and safety glasses, if you had safety glasses. After thirteen years. (Sighs.)

Panic. I never dreamed they'd do it. I really didn't. I still, when I even think of it today it's amazing. I just never dreamed they would.

When we hired into GM they told us we would only be working a little over a year to a year and a half and we ended up going twenty-five months. We were already warned before we worked.

I was one of the lucky ones. I was about three weeks without an unemployment check by the time I hired into General Motors. I made it. It was an experience I'm glad I had. I really am. I wished I had it back. I liked my job [at GM].

They called me in to take the test. At that time the Owosso M.E.S.C. was open. They set me up for April 11, I think it was. I took my testing then and they told us it would be two weeks and we'd get our test results back and a call, or come in and check.

They told us then, Well, in about a month you'll hear from GM. And I chuckled, because I was forty-seven, first of all, and I thought that would be against me. But within a month I was working.

When we hired into General Motors, the only way you could get in was by taking a test. You had to take this aptitude test. That's the only way they'll hire now. You can be the president of the company's grandson, but if you're going to hire in the factory, you're going to have to go through the procedures.

So, there's a lot of people in there with ten years who don't know how to read and write. Really and truly. So they're giving free classes, you know, GED. So I think they're really trying.

When they were getting ready to close our [GM] plant, it was something that was hanging over our head. It was almost a relief when it was over. Not because I wanted to be without a job, but it was like, every day it would be: Was this going to be it? 'Cause they were giving us different dates all the time.

I can't speak for any other plant but Truck and Bus, and when we went in we were told that we'd be laid off. So, I mean, as far as I know, the people who were in the shop longer had to be aware of it. They had to be. But it was still, right up until the end, I mean right up until our last day of work, you had your diehards that said they'll never close this. They'll never shut this plant down.

Because we were running the line from Canada. We were running one whole line of their trucks. And we did military trucks. And they did this speech on TV that they were the best military trucks they'd ever had built at Truck and Bus, but it was already too late.

But the foremans. I felt so sorry for them because they were just as frantic and they were going for interviews to Pontiac and all this kind of stuff and they didn't know what was going to happen to them. And these were foremen, you know. It was just the same. And it's harder to get a job as a foreman, really.

The second time I was, I think, more upset, because I had gotten in and gotten such a good job. And I know, unless they do a complete turn around, that I'll never get into General Motors again.

So I think I was more upset.

I knew this was really over. And I knew then that I'd never get a job that paid as good. And I had a good job. I had to do every truck. Other than the short box trucks and they run very few of them. I'd just start from the front and work to the back. I did the trim. I was on the tailgate. I had to use an air gun. It was a job that you couldn't double up on this one or anything because it was too much work. I had to do every truck. But it was a job that nobody else wanted so I didn't have to worry about somebody else taking it.

That's the job I hired in on. All I did was trade sides. I hired in on the right side and I switched to the left side. You didn't have to look busy, you were busy.

I think first of all, when I first heard I was to be laid off at GM, depression starts. Because you know this is it. There's not going to be another chance.

And I think what irritates me the most of all is the people that go in every day and work—never miss a day, never tardy—are the ones that are out on the street. The jokers that are there four days out of a week or every other week are the ones that stayed. And I mean that from the bottom of my heart.

I think this is the bitterness because all the people who missed their time are the ones that are still working. They had the seniority.

Now, I relate to the Fisher people, more like when the Smeltzer plant closed. Because that was the last thing I ever dreamed would happen, that they'd close. I went around for three months in a state of shock over that. I still say, today, it's still just as big a thing. They locked us out. They just closed the whole plant.

We never got any farther than just where we went to hand in our badges. That was it. That is sad.

It is depressing. But you've got to get into something. If you're just going to sit home and worry about it . . . It's a worry because you've got . . . It was a big let down for us. I could have done a lot of things with that money. Then all of a sudden, it's gone. And then your 26 weeks of unemployment goes fast. My SUB-pay went a lot faster than what I thought it would go. Now, when I first got laid off, SUB-pay was 1.25 credits and my last check was 3.3. It went a lot quicker. Before my unemployment did.

But being laid off from General Motors, there's a lot of opportunities that GM has given me that I didn't have from Smeltzer's. There's schooling. I guess it's right around $3,000 that I have earned that will pay for schooling. If I would have signed up when I was still working, it would have been $5,500. Okay. I didn't sign up until after I was laid off. So I'll only get about $3,000, which is still better than nothing. I am waiting to hear on the second computer class.

General Motors, I think, offers their people a lot of things.

They've got drug abuse centers. They've got your alcoholic centers. Most of the people don't go for the help until they're ready to
be fired. Then they do. But they've got counseling for marriage.
They've got all kinds. And they stipulated to us, that this will
continue. Even though we are on layoff. We can still use all those
services.

Now, when I went to the Human Resource Center, they've
got information up on the bulletin boards. If you're having credit
trouble, that there is a place to come to; they will try to help you
with your credit. So, I think that they've bent over backward to
help people. Now, when Smeltzer's closed their doors, they gave
us nothing. I mean, that was it. I've had two situations.

General Motors is offering a lot, which I think is really good
because when they closed the doors on us at Smeltzer's we didn't
get anything.

And they told everybody, our union rep told us: Keep in
contact. If you move, let them know if your address had been
changed, if you need help, let them know, maybe they can help.
Keep in touch with your union. Don't just drop it because you're
laid off.

I think General Motors has done really well to give us all
this stuff to the people free. And I wish a lot more people would
have gone to this; I think they would have felt better about this.
Like the one lady told us, she said to go to a lawyer or to go to
someone who is qualified to make you out a resume. It's about
$50. They [HRC] will do it all for free and even teach you how to
write your resume.

I mean, I've gone to all these. I've gone the route.

You get there and you listen to these other people. I think
this is a big help—to realize that you're not the only one. And I
feel I'm much better off than a lot of others.

I decided on computers because I think that's the only way
to go. There's so many jobs in that. I went to every one of the
meetings they had when we were first laid off at the Human
Resource Center. And then we went to a school, down off of Van
Slyke, a regular high school to sign up if we wanted to go to work
centers. I went over and signed up for job placement, because I'm
out of everything now. I'm out of SUB-pay and unemployment. I
have nothing coming.

And I went over and signed up for job placement over at the
M.E.S.C. on Van Slyke.

But I told them I'd be willing to take any kind of schooling
that they'd offer. I took one class last semester in computers. And

I'm waiting now for the advanced. And if they don't have one through the high school, I'll start next fall.

I know there's a lot of people upset about this. But on the other hand, a lot of people never went to the meetings. I was amazed at all of the training periods they've had, the talks they've had, the people that just . . . I think they were afraid they might get a job and not draw all of their SUB-pay.

There was not a big turnout at the orientation classes. That's what amazed me.

I think there were, like, six hundred people who were able to keep a job and they're all done as of last week. Because all of the inverse seniority people are going to have to be back on their job. So this is why everyone that was kept are now going to be out.

But I think a lot of people were so afraid that they were going to find a new job quickly. And there is no job out there. There is none. They said, "Well, I want to draw everything I can get." And I said, "Well, you're not going to get a job right away. It's going to take a long time. There's got to be training and everything."

I want to learn how to write a resume and this kind of stuff. These are things that, you know, education never hurts anybody. And you might just as well go. And that was what was so amazing. That people didn't.

I'm not going to go to school for five or ten years. In eight years, Max [husband] retires and I will retire if I'm lucky enough to get another job.

We started out taking classes, just orientation classes, letting us know what was going on, what we could take and use. And the amount of people who never showed up was unbelievable. It was really just like: I don't want to know. I don't care or whatever. And I think a lot of people go through that: I don't care.

I'd like something to get into that takes even a couple years of schooling. But the way they talked, computers are the way to go.

I've worked for seventy-five cents an hour. I've worked hard when I was in school at a duck farm, cutting off chicken legs, five hundred an hour, and turkey legs, we only ran three hundred of those. I only had to do three hundred of those an hour. That was during every other leg. Two of us doing them. I've done lots of jobs. I've got an application in a place right now, and I've been over a couple of times and reminded them that I'm interested.

But everybody says, Well that's five or six dollars an hour. I think that's still good. I've made $8.50 down here when I worked at Smeltzer's and it was good. We had good benefits. Matt has insurance.

It's just that I've always worked. I'm not sure how I'm going to feel not working. Because it wasn't that long after Smeltzer's that I got into GM. I'm not sure how it would be not to work. You know what I'm saying? This is what I think is more scary.

I've always done shop work or grocery work. I have thought about going down to Dells [Durand grocery store] and putting my application in. And I have even thought about going out to Durand Convalescent Center because they are taking applications. But I'm just going to hold off for a bit more because I would like to get into something different.

But there's still a lot of people with that same attitude. *I'm here for the pay and this is it.* These are the people that have hurt the industry, really.

People have to realize, too, that the economy is based on General Motors wages; it always has been. And my husband works on the railroad. He hasn't always made General Motors wages, okay? We've paid for the groceries, same as they have.

But I think a lot of them have never worked other than for General Motors and they're not going to take a job for anything less. And there's not another job out there like that.

I said, If I got a job for five or six dollars, I'm not going to kick. That's still better than sitting back, getting nothing.

There's not anything out there. You're not going to get another job like GM. I think this is what everybody was so mistaken about.

These people who thought they were going to hurt their SUB-pay benefits by looking for work really did hurt themselves because they didn't start looking.

And I think a lot of people thought, Oh, I've got twenty-six weeks of unemployment and it went fast. It really did. It went really fast. SUB-pay didn't last as long. And then everybody was just sure that they were going to get an extension. Well, we went through that when I was working at Smeltzer's. And there was no extension. I got laid off July 9. They closed the door. And I hired into GM in May. So I've never had this long a gap in employment. It is hard.

Like I bought the car through GM when I was working and I would like to be able to pay it off. After my granddaughter leaves, this house is going to be quiet. I've never been that long without being . . . In our house it's not his check or my check. They go together and they pay whatever. Just that knowing that you can't pitch in some money to help, it's a different feeling.

Just standing in that unemployment line with all the other people was really something. I first thought, Oh, all these people are from General Motors. And it was amazing. They weren't. They were from all the other places.

I waited for two and a half to three hours and it's not just GM there. It's the Seven Up Bottling Company people. The bitterness because they brought in part-time seasonal employees and let the full-time go. And Woolworth's sold out. I met this lady who had umpteen years in from Woolworths. It sold and they brought in their own people.

Like one man I talked to three weeks ago, he said, "I have traveled for the Seven Up Bottling Company. I have gone to Mexico and worked for three years. And now, they've hired in seasonal help this past summer and they're letting us go." He had like, fifteen, eighteen years in. He said, "And they're letting us go and keeping the seasonal help because they don't have to pay benefits, holiday pay, and insurance."

And now, when I got laid off, we didn't even have to go to the unemployment office. They brought the unemployment office people into the shop. Now, that was unusual.

I'm not naming names, but I was told when we hired into Truck and Bus that they were told a long time ago that if they didn't bring up their quality, they were going to be without a job. And their attitudes are rotten. Oh, yes. They were told by management. That if they didn't get their quality up . . . And our foremans told us our quality was up the best it's ever been but it was too late. They'd already started the plant in Fort Wayne.

I was driving back and forth to Indianapolis because our daughter's husband was stationed in the service there. So, I've watched that Fort Wayne Truck Plant start from scratch. And I told Matt, I said, "It doesn't make any difference. These people have got to realize this is what they're telling them." And we hired in with that.

So I knew and I was just thankful for the amount of time I got in. I can understand these other people. And then, they kept bringing them in from all the other shops. We had Buick people. There was one night that two fellows worked across from me that were from the Lansing Oldsmobile plant. They had been laid off and sent to Buick.

I've got a girlfriend in town, here. She worked with me at Smeltzer's and hired in to Truck and Bus before I did. She's younger than I am. She's got four kids and I think they're all in school, yet. She took schooling to be a foreman. And she was a foreman when they were laid off.

But she said that her husband worked at Buick and he's got I don't know how many years in Buick City. He's laid off. She had one-half check yet. And she said, "When we're done. I don't know what we're going to do."

They're living in the fifthwheel [trailer]. It's an old one, but they're living in her in-laws' backyard. And they've put a shed on it and a little woodburner to help, too. And she's not working and he's not. Now, she just went over to take another class.

They're paying on their trailer and they've got the kids in school yet. So, I mean, you know, at least Max is working. He got transferred from Birmingham to Pontiac and has got a lot more miles. But. And he's got thirty-one years.

The first class we went to at the HRC I thought was a big flake. It was from Pontiac and we took our class for computer and they said they could only take like twenty people.

They came right out and told us that they didn't think the people from the Flint/Saginaw area were going to drive all the way to Waterford or Clarkston for the training. And I told them, I said, "My husband drives every day from Durand to Pontiac, so, if you really want to do it, you're going to do it."

This one from Pontiac said they were a placement service. And the guy said that if they don't place them, they don't get the money. I don't think they were really interested in taking from our neck of the woods. They wanted more the Pontiac/Detroit area.

When we were having all of our discussions, one of the things that was brought up was: The union doesn't care whether they open or close because they're still going to get their money. And I said, Well, that's what's sad. Because with the Mexico plant, there was no way we could ever compete. In Mexico they were working for $5. You can't get that in Michigan or any state and live on that. Now they've brought it up better. You can't live on $5 a day here.

My friend just took a test last Thursday through the Mott Foundation to take a computer class. So she said there was, like, forty-five people there. Out of the forty-five there was three classes: accounting, data processing, and computer, I think. But she said they're only going to take twenty people in each, three different testings.

We've got a small ceramics business. We were pouring molds this morning. So this is another thing we're doing. I'm teaching ceramics classes. I've got other things that would be interesting to do. Maybe that's why I've adjusted.

When we started our business, we bought two businesses

out and then we added our own molds. We've got a good setup downstairs. I give classes right now, twice a week.

The ceramics business used to be larger until I went to work in the shop. I used to teach ceramics four nights a week. I'm just gradually getting it built back up. It was just a hobby. I took classes in it.

We've been in business ten years. So I do have something. We've got three kilns and a firing table, lots of molds. I want to get my inventory and taxes and that stuff on the computer. Now I take my printout off the computer up here and take it downstairs. We've had our sales tax license . . . (trails off).

That's one of the things I got the computer for is the business.

Our business is the general ceramics. It's called M and S Ceramics. And that gets me out with people. I just can't sit. I've always worked with people. My folks had a small grocery store and I've just always been around people. I'm the oldest of nine children, so. That gets you around people.

And we've got kids with us still. Grandkids. We've got three but they're all married, all in the service. Two in Germany, one in Norfolk, Virginia. But we have this granddaughter with us. She's been with us since she was two and a half months old, so it's like having my own again. But she's leaving in February. So I really have to have something going, because otherwise I wouldn't be able to take it.

We keep busy. I really think that this is the main thing for people. Like the one lady I was talking to, she said, "I just don't know what I'm going to do." And I said, "Why don't you do volunteer work for a while? Get out." She was one of the older ladies. And I said, "Just get out and do something."

With General Motors paying for schooling, people would be foolish not to take them up on it. Now, when I took my computer class, we filled out the papers, sent them in, and before our class started, we had our check back to pay for the class. It was only a hundred dollars, but still.

I have a brother who lives in Nashville and we go there. You can get a job down there if you want to work for minimum wage. But they've got the jobs down there. Here in Michigan, we don't even have that many minimum wage jobs.

But for a person to uproot their whole family and go down to another state and make minimum wage, I don't know how they'd make out.

Start with their schooling and to go to the meetings, I think, is the biggest help for people. Moving out of state isn't a sure thing today. It's just not. My brother had a hard struggle for the first two years down in Nashville and now it's paying off. But it took him a while to get where he is. And it was nip and tuck for quite a while.

I think if they would just go and talk to the other people I think they would be amazed at how much better they'd feel. And just take a few of the classes.

I'm forty-nine, so I don't want to take something that's going to take me a lot of time to get into. But with your schooling, once you've got it, they can't take it away from you. Even if you don't use it, if it doesn't get you a job, you've still got it.

I tell you, my eyes were opened a lot when I went to work there [GM]. I don't know if that was good or bad, but. (Laughs.) No, I worked with a good bunch of people.

I've really learned you're never too old. I've learned that. You're never too old to learn. And you're never really too old to get a job. If you're willing to give it your all. I was forty-seven when I hired into GM after Smeltzer's.

But I've always been in good health because I've always kept busy. That's the main thing. I think you've just got to keep busy. I knit, I've got patterns over there . . . an afghan I've started for my mom.

We've kept busy. He works real hard—Max does the pouring and the firing for the ceramics. I take out the molds and stuff. I just think that you've got to . . . One of the things when you're laid off, you don't have the money to do and go a lot. But there's a lot of things that you can do at home. There really is.

And I don't mean the television set, either. There are a lot of things you can do. Now, we plant a garden every year. And just planning for what you're going to do. It's either feast or famine. When you've got the money you don't have the time and when you've got the time you don't have the money.

The sad thing is the people who think they'll be called back, because GM's going to have to do a lot for that to happen and I think those people might just as well forget it.

Right now, I can't see where General Motors, or any of them—Ford, Chrysler—will do well because there's too many people out of work. It's got to come back and hit the sales. It's got to because who's going to buy the cars? Most people who buy new cars, they've got a $400 car payment. So if you're unemployed, you're not going to.

People that have always made General Motors wages, when they hired in out of high school, those people are the ones who are going to have the biggest adjustment. I went to Union Awareness while I was working. I took all the classes I could take. A lot of people stuck their head in the sand and just didn't pay attention. You got paid for going to it, you didn't have to go to work. And they were interesting. We went two days. The union rep even told us, he said, "There was a time when my grandfather worked at General Motors. My dad worked at General Motors. I got into General Motors, but my kids are joining the service because there's no job at General Motors."

All three of our kids are in the service, so we know how that goes, too. And they might just as well stay in because there's nothing out here.

They also showed us the movie on the big strike—the sit-down strike—and that was interesting. But the union guy there said, We always said if we couldn't buy American-made, we would never use it. But I am very sorry to say I have to turn on this VCR and this TV and they are not made in America." He said, "You cannot buy a TV today that's made in America." And I didn't know that.

Now, on TV recently they interviewed three fellows. Their plant was closed down, I think in Bay City. They were sent to another state, moved their families, and now that plant is closing and there's not another place to send them. So they were really quite discouraged. They had made the change and only got to work a couple of years and now they're out of a job anyway. And they're in another state away from family. So, it's not just a sure thing, you know?

Well, college is so expensive and I think now that kids are getting into it with the idea that you've got to learn something, get in and do something. And other countries have had this. Max's dad came from Germany and he was taught a trade right in school. They were taught a trade besides schooling. You really need something like that today.

I always felt that job security was how you handled your job. If you went to work every day. I'm not one to miss time. I worked twenty-five months over there and I never was tardy and I never missed a day. That's the way I was at Smeltzer's for thirteen years. I think in thirteen years I had maybe ten days counting against me. That, to me, was job security and it's not that way today.

I don't care where you've worked or what you've got, there's no job security.

If you go to work every day, it doesn't make any difference.

15

Zamora

Katherine Zamora is not laid off—not yet. But she does worry about area layoffs. And she has a solution: She owns and operates We Care, a day care center for young children, in addition to working for GM. She is black, forty-five years old, and perfectly coiffed and manicured. She has raised two sons.

I work at GM Truck and Bus Assembly on Van Slyke Road and I've been there for fourteen and a half years. I've been in the trades for almost thirteen years. Small tool repair. I repair air-driven motors.

I'm married, I have two sons. I'm just recently remarried. It'll be four years in May. But I have a son that's twenty-four and I have a sixteen-year-old. And I'm a grandmother.

I started out with prerequisites for an RN. Then I got into college to go through the RN training. I was making more money in the shop, so I dropped it.

So then I had had some courses at Mott. I went to school for the trades at Mott Adult, but I said, I really want a degree. And really, the challenging thing about it is that my brother has finished school and he's got his master's. And my sister is an RN and she's going back for her B.A. And I'm the oldest. So it was really challenging to me. Well, I've got to get this degree.

My sister did say, "You shouldn't let those grades go to waste. You put in a lot of time over there. You've got those credits, you should go ahead and get your degree. You might really want it." I said, "Yeah, I believe one day I will."

And the thing that really ignited me was what my son said to me at breakfast one morning. He said, "Mom, if you're going to go to college and graduate, you better hurry up because I'm going to beat you graduating." (Laughs.)

So I can't just go to school, I've got to show this kid. I've been on the honor roll and maintained a 3.5 average and I said, "Look, kid, I am working and I'm going to school. I clean house. I cook." He and my husband help clean house, that helps me out. But I said, "If I can go to work and wash your clothes and cook your meals and still go to school and be on the honor roll," I said, "What's your problem? All you have to do is go to school, come home, and do little chores."

I'm a member of St. Agnes parish and I'm a part-time student at Mott College. I'm going into child development. I recently opened a day care at Dukette Catholic School, We Care. That's it. I'm the mother. It was a year, January 19.

I've always worked. And I was a single parent for about eleven years. During that time I did everything, worked, everything else came real easy. The only thing that bothered me was things that would relate to my kids.

If things weren't right at home, that kept me tense. I would go to work and I would be there but I wouldn't be there. It made it hard. In one period during that time, my auntie came to live with me and she stayed with me for a while and I was real relaxed. I went to school for the trades and I went to work and everything was fine.

Then she had to go. She wanted to go back down South. So that meant babysitter after babysitter. Then my youngest son, when he first started school, I put him in what was called Young World. It was a day care. And they would take him to his school for a half-day of kindergarten. That was a relief, okay?

So, after working in the trades—I'm the type of person who I get one thing done and I'm always looking for something else. It can be good and it can be bad. Some people say, Well, why don't you just relax? And I say, Well, what do I do if I relax? (Laughs.)

I thought of a number of things that I could do. I could do this or that. But then I said, I want to do something that helps somebody.

I got to thinking about it. I looked into a number of things that I could do. I thought about a restaurant, different things. Then I was talking to someone and they said, "You know, what about day care? Have you ever thought about day care?" I don't even remember who it was that I was talking to. I said, "No, I never thought about that." I was teaching a religious class up at St. Agnes. And I really love kids.

And then reading all the articles about child abuse and things like that. That was a great factor, also. Well, I started looking into it. I spoke to the principal of Dukette at the time, Bill

Moran. And he said, "Why don't you check with Father [priest at St. Agnes], we've got plenty of room here. Open up a day care here on the school grounds."

Then I spoke to Father about it and he said that someone had attempted to do it before. I don't know what problems they ran into, but they had everything for the licensing and everything but they didn't carry it through.

So I went to the library and I started taking out books about day care and I went to Four C's and I talked to people and asked about things. Then I spoke with the lady who owns the Pied Piper and I talked with her. She was my instructor at Mott in my child development classes. I had met her a few years ago when I was in Mary Kay Cosmetics. She had come to one of our meetings.

Somehow, everything started falling in place, you know. She said, "Well, I'll help you any way I can." She was more or less like a catalyst. She was very instrumental.

Then I went to different day cares, visiting them. Talked with some of the directors. And I went to Cedar Street, to Gerber on Clio Road. Then I went to Holy Rosary, because it's Catholic and I was going to be in a Catholic setting. And I went over to Blessed Sacrament and they had one there.

The lady there was very good because she had just started out herself. I did all my fieldwork. What's all involved in it, what I'd need, and how to get started. I had a million and one questions so I just started out by more or less touching bases with people and reading as much as possible on it.

Then I worked with a group of ladies called the HUB Committee. It started over a year ago. It was sponsored through the Mott Foundation, the Chamber of Commerce, and some other organization. Anyway, it was a group of us who got together to form this committee. We were helping women who wanted to become entrepreneurs. They had helped quite a bit. Working with them I had some idea how to get set up, what to do, and where to go. That was very instrumental.

Then this other group called the Flint Businesswomen Development, I was on that board, too. So, everything just fell into place at the right time.

That was basically the groundwork. But the hard part was getting everything for licensing. I'm telling you, they check you out. I was going to Mott and I really appreciate it now because I feel like it was real helpful.

You have your regular forms you fill out for licensing, but you have to get your staffing together. I had to draw a blueprint—a layout—of the day care and what it was like. She had me do all that. She sent me material about how I had to get with a supplier for preschool furniture. I had to do all that and all the time I'm working and I'm going to school at Mott.

I did double work in school because I was doing exactly the same thing in my classes as I had to for the center. It was double. She asked for different things in my class. So, I had to draw two plans.

Then we had to wait for fire doors to be put up because we were in the basement of the school. Licensing requires that the fire inspector has to come out. Health Department. I had to pass all these people.

But now I know that everything is up to standard and I don't have to worry about that. That's the good part about it. My teacher was coming to check on me one day and I met her at the door and I was so tired that my whole body was just . . .

She said, "How are you doing?" And I said, "My whole body is tired. Even my tongue is tired!"

The few women friends that I have, they thought it was great. They just can't believe I could do it, you know. How can you do all this?

But most of the guys that I work with didn't even know that I did that. I didn't even talk about it to them. I just . . . some things, I don't know. It's not that I didn't want to brag, because I look at things as blessings. And I look at every day as a blessing. Having health and being able to accomplish things is a blessing to me. It comes from God, not me.

But people look at it differently. Especially guys when you go in and you work in trades. Well, working in the shop in the first place, most of the men feel like you're treading on their ground, you know. *You're doing a man's job, what are you doing here? You should be at home having babies and taking care of kids. Why don't you give that job up so some young man can have it?*

And I say, Well, you know, this is my job and some young man is going to have to find his, okay?

When you run into guys like that, how could I say? How could somebody cheer you on when they really don't want to see you do anything?

So my family and my close friends were the ones who really gave me the incentive to keep going. And they were the ones I was glad to share it with. But the guys that I work with—they were the last to know.

And I tell you, when I first went into trades, I was on the line and I was going to school for RN and the biggest response that I got from the ladies on the line—and I would talk to the ones who were around my job—I said I was going to school and they said, "What do you want to do that for? You got a job here in the shop." I said, "No, you should do it, too." They said, "Girl, how can I do that?" I said, "Easy. Just decide that you're going to do it, pray, and go at it. Don't stop to think about it."

That's the hardest thing. If I stop and take tally I get tired. (Laughs.) You know that saying, busy people get things done? It's true.

It was depressing to me if I go out and, like, with myself being motivated or whatever and I would talk to different girls in the shop about going to school, even trying to get into the trades, you know. They said, "Girl, I don't have time for that."

Well, my youngest son is asthmatic. Between school, work, I was at the hospital maybe two or three times a week when he had an asthma attack. Each time I'd just think, Well, keep right on going. Because it was just another thing, another day in my life. And that's just the way I saw it.

But I would go to work at 4:00, 4:30 in the evening and get off at 1:30, 2:00 in the morning. Come to think of it, I've been doing this for quite a while. So, when they said they didn't have time . . .

I like going to school. I love learning. I do. But some people don't want to grow.

It's a burning desire I have. I had a guy tell me one time that pretty women are dumb. Ha. That most pretty women were dumb. They go on looks. That was challenging for me. (Laughs.)

Okay, what really gets me is: Okay, you have this twenty-nine-year-old lady who doesn't want to do anything with her life and have you looked at people who really can't do anything with their lives?

At one time in my life I lived on ADC and it was a little less than $200 a month. I lived in a low-income apartment with two kids. My husband had left me and that's all I had. Okay? Just us. My parents are here, but I've never wanted my parents to take care of my kids.

There I was with two kids. I had to stop working. At the time I was a secretary and I had to stop working because my youngest son was having problems with his asthma. Every time I'd go to work, I had to come home. We didn't know at the time that he had asthma. We just thought he was premature; he weighed three pounds when he was born. We just thought it was complications.

So I had to come home and stay with him and all of a sudden my husband just left. And there I was with two kids. And I was in a neighborhood. I would get up early in the morning and clean my apartment up. Then I'd go and visit with the ladies there in the complex.

I got to know a lot of people. I touched life with those people. I got a chance to learn how to appreciate everything that I had. Because there were ladies that didn't have anything hardly. And some of them were really illiterate. They didn't know how to read or write.

Look at the GM-UAW tuition. Girl, I love it. I love it. Nowhere else on earth could I do that. Do you understand what I'm saying?

When I was on ADC before I just had the one son and I had been sick and I wasn't working. I was separated and the caseworker came and told me that they would pay for the money to get into school, the money for my classes. I got right in it. I went to Baker's. I got a clerk-typist certificate from there. That was back in 1971.

But, see, I've always had the feeling you just never learn enough. I don't feel that you can. And then I want to share it. Every time I get it, I share it with someone.

What I learned at Baker's, as far as the business part and running things, all of that comes into the day care center, too. All of it has just—it's the molding of oneself.

But my husband has been such a great asset and I just thank God for him. He's a one-man cheering section. And he's there for me. When you're as energetic as I am and my husband is nowhere near as energetic as I am. We're complete opposites. But the thing of it is, he doesn't stop me. Before I always had that type of man. This is my third marriage. It was like I had to compete.

The first time was hard because it lasted nine years, but the second one, I said, I cannot waste my time. I cannot afford to lose what I have accomplished and I will not let anybody stop me from doing what I know is good for me.

You have those people that will hinder you.

I've had John say, "Don't you have something to do?" Because I'm always gone. And I'll think, This is terrible. And he'll say, "Don't you have anything to do today?" That's like saying, It's all right, go ahead.

You know, you can sit and think of all the bad things that has happened to you. And that will stop you from doing anything. Some people look at things as downfalls. I look at them as steps.

Ever since I've been there I've heard there's going to be a big layoff. You're going to get laid off. But guess what? I never put faith in General Motors. I have faith in God. And I always said before I got there, I existed. If General Motors decides to close down, I don't cease to exist. You know what I'm saying?

What really gets me is a lot of times, these young ladies in the shop, they get exploited by the fellows. That's so degrading.

When you're on the line it seems like you have to put yourself in a precarious world in order to survive it. I was always reading. I had to read because if I didn't then I'd have to think about what I was really doing.

I was on the line about a year and a half. The line is running and you have people in there who's done that all their lives. It was like: This isn't a job. I'm not thinking. If I'm where I can't add something to it or give something to it, it's boring. It's very boring for me.

The thing about the layoffs is: How do you orient all these people? Get all of them to realize that they've got to do something different? After so long.

Because I don't know what's going to happen at the Truck plant. My husband and I, we're always talking about what we're going to do when it happens. I told him, "Whenever it happens, I'm going to be working on it. I'm going to be doing two or three different things and when it happens it's just going to happen. It's not going to be the end of me. I'll just do something else."

The good part of that is when you've been poor, you don't really mind going back. Some people do. I'm not afraid of it. It's not a world that I can't survive.

Maybe someone else who has younger children. Some of these people who are going to be laid off right now have been working maybe two years. They've been drawing that big paycheck, all those benefits and then—boom. Not to have anything. See, these are the people who've got to make a decision because they told them that they would never work for General Motors again.

With myself, it's not like having twenty-five or thirty years, but I reaped the good part of it. The classes and things. The vacation and bonuses and all that. It's good. It's good.

The only part I would want to change would have been the management and the people's relationship. That's horrible. I look at supervisors and people more educated than they are and they take their position and they play God.

Can you imagine how hard it is to tell somebody, This is the end of your life as far as we're concerned? This is it.

I think people should do an overall view of oneself. That's the first thing. You've got to know yourself. My likes, my dislikes. That step you have to do. That determines what you're going to do. Not just jumping into anything, but something you'll like. A lot of people start things and then say, Hey, I don't want to do this. But if they had done some soul-searching they wouldn't have that barrier to come up against later.

Then the next step is to utilize their time even if they're not going to go into a business. At least go to school or get into something where they volunteer to do something. Doing something. You can go out and help people. There's a lot of people out there who need help. There's people who just need someone to talk to. There's shelters, soup kitchens and all that.

I find that if I'm taking on a task where I'm helping somebody else, that takes the eye off of me. And if something bad happens to me then I don't have time to look at it because I'm doing something positive.

I tell people I'm a winner even when I lose. Because I'm going to find out how I lost and learn not to do it again.

Griffin

Claude Griffin, a small-boned, slow-talking man in his late-fifties, worked for General Motors at the Buick City plant for ten years. Yoga has always been an avocation of his and since his layoff in October of 1987, he has taught classes at the Corner-stone Yoga Studio. Squatting on a Persian rug in the semi-dark, we spoke just after one of his classes. Alto voices and spiritual music softly wafted from a stereo.

What I'm going to say may mean that you don't want to use me as an interview.

Because I've been doing yoga on the side from my regular job at GM. It's never been successful, financially. I think it could be.

I've been laid off since October, 1987. Worked on the line. Ten years.

It was out of disillusionment, okay? It was in the sixties and I was going to law school, had a lot of personal problems. My family broke up. I went and lived on skid row. On Cass Corridor in Detroit.

I was very despondent. I'd spent time in the military, the Korean War. And I was a heavy drinker, never got on drugs, you know, but . . . When I got out I just couldn't find myself. I mean I think that people who have been in a war really have a difficult time re-establishing themselves in life again. A lot of Vietnamese veterans have found the same thing. It's not just a drug issue.

When you have been trained to kill and your mind has focused on that for a while, life gets kind of cheap. And all the things that you were raised with, like your family and caring for people and love and those things sort of fall in the background.

That's what I felt and I think a lot of people feel that way. I mean, you only work for one reason—to protect and to kill. And it's oriented toward victory. Whatever means it takes.

So when you get out again. I was really disoriented. The friends I grew up with were married or working or something. It wasn't the same world. And it's true you can never go back home again but, you know, it's a shock to not have anyplace to go. It's home but it really isn't.

So, anyway, I went through a long period of trying to figure out what the heck I wanted to do. I thought if I get to be a lawyer, that's a prestigious position and it's money and I will be accepted in the community.

So my idea was to have an office with a Cadillac sitting outside, a beautiful secretary who I might want to take out on the weekend or something, all that stuff. (Laughs.) Really. Shallow.

I thought that was sort of the epitome of life. Financial security and social prestige. A common thing in our society, you know.

Well. After my family broke up and after I'd spent a lot of time drinking, trying to find myself . . . Something kept going on in the back of my mind: What is life all about anyway? What the heck is all this business for?

And I went to different churches, floundered around, and they all seemed like nonsense. Well, I finally got to the point where I just lived for the day, going to the bars, associating with streetwalkers, winos. My girlfriend was a streetwalker. She was a sort of a semi-prostitute.

But there was a certain sense of loyalty there that I couldn't find in real life. I mean, down there it was a daily survival program and you had to have comrades, you know, people you could really trust. So, you would give your last dime to a fellow, because you knew you'd need it yourself the next day or so.

Three years. And I quit school and I got fired from my job. I just wanted to disappear.

It got so bad that I found myself lying in the street, down on Third Avenue. And I didn't know how I got there. And I thought: This is the end. It's either I do something now, or this is curtains. The end of my life.

So I called AA. And these people came and nursed me around. I really couldn't have. I was in bad shape. I had to be hospitalized for a while.

Well, part of the program is a spiritual awakening. In AA. So I pursued that aspect of it as carefully as I could because I knew this was a one-way street from now on. I couldn't go back. I couldn't survive that way again. A life or death situation.

So I searched around—spiritual awakening? What the heck does this mean?

And I went to churches. I went to Central Methodist and I'm glad that the church was there, because they really had some wonderful ministers. I got a lot of help from them.

But I spent a lot of time in public libraries, trying to read in the philosophy and religion section. There'd be a lot of nuns going in there. They read, too, I found out. Priests and other people like me, trying to find what life is all about.

I came across a book called *The Hidden Teaching Beyond Yoga* by Paul Brundt, an Englishman. His writings weren't very well known in those days. But the interesting thing is, he died a few years ago and now his books—I was out at Young and Welshans Booksellers and there's several volumes of his books out there.

For some reason, it really captured my mind. I guess because it had a strong philosophical background. He talked about Emmanuel Kant and John Locke and how our whole system of ideas was built on these things. And I was really impressed with it.

So, you couldn't hardly find books on the occult or mysticism that you can nowadays. This was in the late-fifties.

I mean, there were women in Washington, wives of politicians and congressmen, they'd go to yoga classes in secret.

The only thing that I could find were a lot of books on mysticism like *The Cloud of Unknowing* and *St. John of the Cross*, you know, the dark night of the soul and William Law, I remember his stuff. And, of course, St. Francis of Assisi and St. Ignatius of Loyola, and all these people.

And I'd read a lot of philosophy, but it was much too intellectual. I wanted to get beyond that. To a spiritual awakening. I read a lot of that stuff. And I really wasn't satisfied because it seemed to be couched in traditional ideas so much. And I never forgot that book about yoga.

So I started reading more about Hinduism and it was really hard to find anything. It's incredible how bigoted our society is. The more frustrated I got, the more I started looking for ideas to support my discontent.

And one of the books I found that probably was the real turning point in my spiritual awakening was Percy Bysshe Shelley, an English poet. I read his philosophical notes to the poem, "Queen Mob."

That was really . . . Then I picked up his book, *The Necessity of Atheism* that someone had put together. And they said that he had been expelled from Cambridge for writing that.

So I thought this is the man for me. Exactly what I need. And there was all this protest movement going on, anyway. And I got into all that stuff and I'd been in the war.

I never forget the day I was reading Shelley and I was so enamored by what he was saying. Because, well, his mind was one of the sharpest minds I'd ever encountered, too, I mean his poetry was just—I couldn't imagine how anyone could be so inspired at his early age and so exacting.

Well, his notes after that poem, to me, were the most interesting. He talks about being a vegetarian. He was a vegetarian, too, you know. And he talks about a lot of religious ideas and especially about how Christianity is a warped system of thought.

After reading him, I remember it was such a liberating feeling because I could never get beyond American philosophy, it seemed like. Traditional concepts—Emmanual Kant and all this crap.

I remember I put my feet up on the library table where I was reading, I just felt so rebellious. I just felt like being nonchalant and free for the first time in spite of what anybody thought. Hell.

And I had spent some time reading and reading from the Great Books Foundation. I don't know if you know about that or not. It was this thing started by, I don't remember his name, but Sydney Harris [columnist] used to be a member.

You read certain books from the classics like *Syntapicon*, the *Ptereoptagypita*, Plato, *Apology*. And then you'd get together and discuss them. Try to understand what it really meant in terms of your own life. It was really a wonderful thing.

Makes you realize how much you really don't know. And also, how much you can learn about your own mind and about life. So, anyway, I had my feet up on the table and the librarian said, "Get your feet off that table!" And I just smiled and I put my feet down, okay.

But I felt like I discovered something wonderful. And for a long time I'd go around churches and set people up. It was sort of a process of breaking my own self free from this. Because I had been raised in a fundamentalist tradition.

And I still, in spite of myself, am a little fearful. It was a little hard to shake my mind free from this Christian stuff.

So, I would argue with priests, ministers, all kinds of people, just for the exercise. I didn't mind humiliating people, who wanted to, or whatever. (Laughs.) I remember one time somebody said, "Claude, why don't you leave these people alone?" (Laughs.) It's pretty hard to match someone, you know, when they've had this background of great books, discussion groups every week, and you're reading in philosophy and stuff like that. Unless you're on your toes or have some background.

So that went on for a long time. And I finally lost the sense of challenge and interest for that.

And I think I was started when I met my first teacher, who I thought to be my real spiritual teacher. He's a man from India who was a citizen of this country and married a woman and he lived in Beverly Hills. He was a Sikh, wore a big turban, went all over the country lecturing. One of the most remarkable people I ever met.

And I followed his development for several years. I would even go to the town he'd go to and stay there. He would lecture and he taught meditation. I pursued that life for a long time. And it gradually dawned on me that there had been quite a transformation taking place in me since I quit drinking.

It was about three years now and I hadn't had a drop of alcohol. More than that, it seemed like there was a sense of some divine, I don't know, law or something. Because, in spite of the talk about atheism, I think Shelley is one of the most religious people I've ever met. Even though he talks about it [spirituality] in an atheistic mode.

I had never figured out what I wanted to do yet in my life. I was wondering whether I should go back to law school. I couldn't fit it in with my moral ideas. I felt like most lawyers were charlatans.

I floundered around and started teaching yoga in my home. Taught it for the Flint Board of Education for several years. Taught a yoga class for the University of Michigan, for the Adult Education.

What I wanted to do was open a yoga studio for a long, long time. And I found a building downtown. And I thought, Well, it doesn't cost much, I won't have that much to lose. I'm going to try it. So I moved down here, been here about eight years now. Well, it was about the same time or a few years before that I got my job at GM.

And the problem I've had is that working for GM, you know, you're put on different shifts. I worked nights for a long time. And I went back to UM-Flint, got a degree in psychology. And then I just—I couldn't seem to—I'd get a nice group going here and I'd be put on another shift. So I'd have to let the class go. All the time.

I could never give my full attention to it. So.

I still haven't got it all together. I've been off since October. Flint has changed a lot since then, too. The economy and what have you. So, I don't know. It seems impossible anymore.

But I haven't been able to find a way of having classes on a regular basis so I can support myself. I charge only $3 too. Again, there's moral principle there. I'm not into it for money. I'm into it because I'm still pursuing a spiritual path. I'm trying to benefit people and have money be secondary to that.

For a long time I didn't charge anything. I wouldn't do it. My own teacher never did it. One of the principles is that if a person charges, then it's probably not inspired by God. You know.

But in India, the tradition is that the teacher will always teach free, never ask for money when he's teaching.

I've been here eight years. I don't know how I've survived. Well, I've supported the place mostly through my wages. And like, tonight, there were only four people and there was one person who didn't pay, so that's nine dollars. I haven't even looked, to tell you the truth.

But it's still been a very rewarding experience. I've learned an incredible amount of things just from working with people and interacting with them and from trying to keep a spiritual sense about it. I didn't know all the things I needed to know and I still don't. But I've learned an incredible amount and maybe someday in the near future I might be able to put a place together that really will be prosperous.

I do workshops. I have done workshops here and I charged $10 a session. That was good. I could make maybe enough to survive that way but it's correlated with yoga. The workshops I was giving were on wholistic principles, trying to help people undestand that it's not external circumstances that shapes your destiny so much as it's your response to life.

What is my next step? Good question. My unemployment is going to run out in about a month and I don't know how I'll survive. I'm not making enough money in classes. Um. I guess what I'll have to do is be a street person again or something. I don't know.

Maybe sell the building. But, it's really tough in this area. It's hard to sell a piece of property and not only that, people don't even want to come down here, nowadays. A lot of women from Davison and Grand Blanc won't go downtown.

If I could be on the faculty, make a salary at a university, yeah. They ought to teach yoga at universities, too. As part of their regular program, you know, instead of just as a recreational activity. Because it involves philosophy and so much.

People come here and they have such incredible experiences. I mean, that's why they come. They learn how to relax and let go.

Okay, so I guess I'm just in a period of transition where, again, it's either sink or swim. I'm at that level, now.

There's still this thing in the back of my mind about making a profit, whether I'm going to be oriented toward profit or content, giving something to people that's really good, beneficial, and so on.

There's constant conflict it seems between those two ideals.

Do I think anything at GM helped me? Hm. (Wryly.) Oh, definitely. Yeah.

It's both bad and good. I learned that most of the people who work there, on the surface, are shoprats. They have that mentality of being mechanical. Tell me what to do. They don't want to bother figuring things out, being responsible.

And they are heavy into smoking, eating junk food, and things like that make them sick. But management is glad they are because they're easier to control that way. They provide the machines, you know, where they get the candy and cigarettes and coffee.

I think the whole thing is mindless. Maybe on an unconscious level. But there it is.

It was really a test for me to see how well I could live by the principles of yoga and still work there on the line. It's so dehumanizing.

See, I learned something else, too, about the people who work there. They have a lot of integrity, too. I mean, these are people who grew up just like you and me and were thrown into that miserable situation. And they've learned some extraordinary survival techniques.

And you can really learn a lot of things from those people. It's not formal education, but, by golly, it's very useful.

One of the things I learned was how to deal with management. I had a picnic in there, really. I would take books in. I even wrote a manuscript about that thick [indicates several inches with fingers] when I was in there. I would time it, see. Your job takes maybe so many minutes. You do that and go back. You know the next car is going to be there and you got, say, two minutes to do this, reading or whatever. And then you go back to it.

It's not an easy thing to master, but after a while I learned. I'd take my books in and I could be all alone, see? I could shut the whole world out. And I'd be totally absorbed because you don't have to talk to anybody. It's all manual. Just use your hands. And all the time your mind can be in another place altogether. I wasn't even there a lot of the times.

But when I was there, I was a complete maverick. I mean, I used to just intimidate for the fun of it. I mean, management, they're such . . . dopes. You know? I found out that if I could get a core of people on the line to stick with me, we could control everything. Management. Everybody. The whole factory. I shut down the plant a lot of times.

And we had the committeeman. We could use the committeeman. If the boss tells you not to do something, you say, Well, I want to see the committeeman. And they have to let you see a committeeman. So then you spend another thirty minutes in the office with your feet up on the desk talking to the committeeman and the foreman has to find somebody else to cover your job, you know. (Laughs.) Pretty soon, they don't tell you that.

One time, I remember, they were talking about the Quality of Work Life program. It was just a bunch of crap. So this is what I did. We had a white crayon and you write on the windshield if you found something wrong with the car, what it was.

So, I started writing all kinds of things on the windshields. All kinds of remarks. About the boss and whatever came to mind. It was really intimidating. But I had several people around me who were really getting a kick out of it and they were supporting me.

So this one time, he sent somebody down with a stack of paper, said, "Claude, don't write on the windshields, it's too hard to get off. Write on the paper." So, I started writing on the paper and I'd tape it on the windshield. (Laughs.) They were eight and a half by eleven sheets and then I taped a whole mess of them together, I don't know, twenty or thirty sheets. I had this great, big—it covered the whole car and I wrote all over it and put that on a car. And I finally said, "I'm out of paper! Send me some more paper!" (Laughs.)

You know, just crazy things like that.

And those things . . . What else can you do? When you're there under these dehumanizing circumstances. You're supposed to be this automaton that does the same thing, the same movement, hour after hour after . . . You'd go crazy if you didn't have something like that to do.

One of the most disconcerting things is that the people who work there have given up on life, in a sense. I mean, all of them had aspirations of life when they were growing up. You know, I'll fall in love, and Oh, I'll get a job doing something I like, I'll go into business or something. But after a while, you lose that.

I know some people take the money and do something else and get out. Very few. A few of them do. But for the most part, it's so demoralizing that you're just totally dispirited after awhile. You just give up on faith, hope, finding a good life.

And so, seeing people like that, and seeing how they function after that, the people who decide to stay there until they retire. It's interesting how they're surviving. The survival techniques they've learned. How they're going to cope with this.

You get into that routine, you know. You go home and you're really not home, because you have to get ready to go back to work the next day. And whatever you do is geared to that. So it's like you're living in this artificial world. Which is not really related to anything that's really going on out here.

My goal was to find the easiest job in there so I didn't have to work any harder than I had to. So that I could devote most of my time to what I really wanted. And I read most of Jane Austen's novels in there. Dostoevsky. (Laughs.) I read Albert Camus. The myth of Sisyphus. (Laughs.)

But I knew what my limits were. I was called in the office one time. I developed this . . . Yoga really helped me. I learned that nobody could really intimidate me if I didn't want them to. I could watch my breathing, you know, and keep my outer composure. Because I spent a lot of time in meditation and practicing breathing, postures.

I remember one time the general foreman and my foreman had me in an office. He said, "Claude, you've been placed on a sacrificial altar. We're going to make an example of you." And I sat there looking out the window. And they said, "What have you got to say about that?" And I wouldn't say anything. Like they weren't even there. (Laughs.)

So they finally, they really got frustrated and one jumped up and said, "What have you got to say?" And I said, "I want to see the committeeman." Simple things like that.

I was escorted out by plant protection one time. Because I told the foreman to go fuck himself. I whispered it in his ear while he was talking to the plant superintendent. Another time the general foreman said to me, "Claude, you used to work at General Motors but you don't anymore." I said, "Kiss my ass." Just like that, you know. And I started walking away and he said something and I turned around and I said, "Kiss my ass." That was the end of it.

Well, anyway, after a while I got a reputation. I mean, every member of management knew me and they knew that I was pretty smart and that they had to be careful how they dealt with me. They were kind of frustrated as to what to do with this guy. So, after a while, they would try to just pacify me. Anything. Give me the easiest job, whatever.

And I had a reputation with fellow workers, too. When they

had a problem, they'd come and talk to me and say, What are we going to do about this? I became an advisor for a lot of people. They used to call me the Professor. Even people in the union got to know me and I could get almost anything I wanted. Call the committeeman. He'd take me off the line and we'd just sit down and shoot the breeze.

I have a lot of respect for the people who work in the factories. Like you would have respect for someone who'd been living in abject poverty and learned to survive. Like the people I chummed around with on skid row. It's a very demeaning lifestyle. But they really had some survival techniques developed. And I really felt loyal to those people. I really admired them. There's a sort of rebellious reaction there, too. Rejection of authority.

The training programs . . . I don't know if those people are really in touch with the unions, the men on the line and what I believe to be the important things about it. Part of the reason the people are trapped in the factory in the first place is their own . . . It's their own fault, I mean, in the sense that, you know, they're smoking, they're eating all kinds of junk food. They're keeping their physical energy level low. And they don't have some mode or way of responding to life that gives you energy, inspiration, creativity, and things like that. Like, Lay me off, I've had enough of this.

Those people feel helpless. Because they're still doing all these things that reinforce it. Like smoking marijuana, drinking, and whatever.

For practical purposes, from the individual's viewpoint, I think that self-esteem is fundamental. Doing something that, after you've done it, you can say, I'm glad. I feel proud of myself for building this, writing this, making this, whatever. At GM you don't have it. If you do, you're an unusual person.

I think we can do a lot to help people achieve in their lives. Help them see why self-esteem is important. The reason they're into drugs and smoking and stuff like that is they both feed on each other. Being on the line is a dehumanizing situation and smoking and drugs are on the other side.

I think that a person needs to come to terms with themself and realize if they don't do something that they really love to do, enjoy doing, they'll probably be doing something like working in the factory, that they really hate. Because everybody has to survive.

I think one needs to realize that external circumstances are not the controller in our lives. They are created by us, as a matter of fact. If we realize that, then we're not a victim anymore. We know that we have the freedom to choose and by making choices, we create different circumstances or more desirable circumstances.

Find something that you really feel competent doing. It's not a simple, easy task to do. It takes a lot of processing and maybe one time you find something that you think is just for you and you'll change your mind and so on. But the important thing is to at least have a goal and have a defined process for achieving goals in the best possible circumstances.

A person has to realize that what they may decide to do or determine to do may not necessarily be profitable. It may not be the thing to make them rich. But it's still rewarding and they can still enjoy life. Maybe the wealth would be an encumbrance, anyway.

Then, the other thing I try to do is to link these things to the study of yoga. Emphasize the importance of diet. The food you eat becomes the cells of your body, the bones. So, if you eat junk, you know. (Laughs.) You won't have that much energy and you won't feel like putting forth that extra effort you might need. More than that, you won't have a sense of well-being that you have when you walk out on a spring day and have the energy, the attunement to life. When you've been out the night before drinking and you've been up that same morning eating donuts, drinking coffee, listening to the news and a lot of people are getting murdered and all this, your energy is sapped.

So, diet, nutrition is important, physical exercise. We teach breathing exercises, postures. It's a very wholesome kind of exercise. Not like aerobics or anything else demanding. And we teach meditation. How to let go of the tension in one's mind. Just laying down, for example, is not necessarily being relaxed. Being relaxed is surrendering the guilt, the fear, resentment, anger. Things that are locked in your subconscious that haunt you sometimes at night. Or even in your daily work that restrict you.

We work with those things and couple that with designing goals. Learning to channel energy. Whatever we're expressing, it's a form of energy. Whether it's anger, writing a poem, worrying. That's all an expression of energy. Very often we feel like we have no control over how that energy is expressed. We teach people to identify that emotion and use it more productively.

What is needed is the basic things like art, philosophy, maybe, or something that gives you a sense of developing self-esteem. Knowing that life has a meaning personally, that you're really useful to yourself and other people. That's grounded in the things that philosophers have been talking about for centuries. And the artists are experts at it. That's why they're known. Because they do have self-esteem. They won't sell their souls to an industry.

It's really important to work, but to work for something that's good and beneficial.

Nobody wants to work in the factories, not if they've been in there for a while. They see that it's stupid. The whole thing is crazy. Even from management's viewpoint. They're not being efficient. It's like a mental institution. Nobody knows what the hell they're doing, hardly. They make cars. But, so what? The Japanese are doing it better than we are.

I think that we need to go back to those basic things and try to understand: What the hell is life for, anyway?

17
Hamper

Ben Hamper, also known as "The Rivethead," has written for the Michigan Voice, Esquire, Mother Jones, *the* Detroit Free Press *and other publications during his ten and a half years working on the line for General Motors.*

Former Michigan Voice *editor Michael Moore gave Hamper his start at professional writing. Hamper first did music reviews, then he wrote about life at General Motors.*

The Rivethead was a persona Hamper created for talking about what happens on the line. Although not currently laid off, he has written much on the experience of working on the line. Some of his writing was actually done in the shop with longer articles completed during subsequent layoffs. To me, he represents the "diverse population" mentioned in this book's introduction.

Hamper's I'm-just-a-shop-rat demeanor is set to belie his intimate knowledge of every con job, rhetoric, jargon, and scam in the books, including poetry books. His favorite poets include Charles Bukowski and Michigan poets Diane Wakoski, Danny Rendleman, and Jim Daniels, who writes about working and workers in factories. "I was almost ashamed to say that I was a writer about the plant. Because [Jim Daniels] verbalized so well in that poetry. Just the mundane, just the everyday little situations. The beer after work in the tavern. The kind of lifestyle. I remember he had a poem about his brother who worked first shift, left him a six pack of beer on the seat. Just shit like that. When I read that stuff I felt totally destroyed because he was verbalizing just exactly what I was feeling.

"I can't do the poetry like that. I'd read it and say, There's no damn reason why I shouldn't be able to come up with this,

because I'm operating on the same basis he was. Oh, there's not a wasted word in his stuff."

In addition to being named one of Esquire's Men of the Year, Hamper has been interviewed on ABC's "Today Show." His picture also appeared on the front page of the New York Times as part of a story on blue-collar writers.

He hosts a late-night rock show on public radio station WFBE.

"We've been doing it . . . it'll be six years in February. It's on from 12:00 to 1:30 every Saturday night.

"Really, that's my first love, right there. Rock music. I still keep up with the shit that's popular with fourteen-year-olds. Hard core. Speed core.

"Oh, there's so many young bands out there. At this time, there's at least as many good bands as there was in 1969, '68. People are always so anxious to sit around and mope and say, Oh, wow, when we were growing up, man, we had Hendrix and the Doors and we had . . . Fuck with all that. There's bands just as good. It's just that radio has clamped down.

"The Dead Jacksons. The Dead Milkmen. The Smiths.

"The stuff we tend to play is quite aggressive. Violent mixed in with a generous stew of golden garage hits of the '60s. We try to make it just as noncommercial as we possibly can. If it can't be played on radio, it will be on our show.

"Even 'My dad's a fucking alcoholic,' by the Frantics, we played a few times."

During the reorganization of General Motors plants in Flint, Hamper was moved to the Pontiac plant where he still works.

Well, I wasn't even laid off. I was on a medical leave. Had to leave, actually.

So you went back December 21, then?

Yeah. I'd been off since about May. And during that period, I'd been transferred from Flint to Pontiac.

I'd heard that some have been laid off from there.

Yeah, a lot of them are. Matter of fact, next week, they're laying off a whole bunch of these new people I just met. Just get to know them and then they're going to be gone next week.

But you're still working. How long have you worked there?

For GM? Ah, ten and a half years.

Have you been offered the Golden Handshake?

No, I would have grabbed that and I'd be gone.

I haven't been in a position where my plant or my security with the plant was that fragile that they would offer it. But if they would, by chance, I'd take it. 'Cause I want to get out of there.

What is going on, what are you seeing?

All I know about is the rivet line. Ask me about the rivet line. I can't give you broad answers on the effects on the workers' minds and all that.

But I could tell you about the sadness of going back there three weeks ago and visiting the old crew on the rivet line. There was only maybe four guys out of twenty-five that were still left.

And I said, "Where's Hogjaw? Where's Herman? Where's Michael? Where's Big Red?" And the two or three or four guys that were left said, "Well, he got it shortly after you left." "He got canned last week." "He was gone two months ago."

It just feels like the disintegration of a family unit because these people you work with . . . especially the guy next to you. We doubled up on jobs. You see more of this person than you do of your wife.

And at times we'd call each other, kiddingly, jokingly, "Sweetheart," ha! We worked second shift and I would see a lot more of Paul Schroeder than anybody. Who, outside of the plant, I know nothing about but inside the plant we were husband and wife.

So it's hard when you see those people go past.

But the good parts. It's like married couples. Where do you work? Eight or nine or ten hours a day next door to some guy and you help each other out and work out a little gig where you double up on jobs. And one guy reads the paper for a while while one guy does it. And you just come into this . . . beautiful . . . relationship; obviously, it's not marriage, but it's as close as you can get. "Man-to-man," you know.

But then, all of a sudden, one day it stops. Schroeder. I went out on sick leave and I came back and Schroeder was gone. And I gotta' admit, it hit me in the heart. Almost like your wife left you. Wasn't a romantic thing. I was just so destroyed by it, to think

that I could do my job now without Paul. And he was an extension of me for all these times.

We had the same code words, and it'd be so noisy and I could
go just like this (moves his hand) and he'd know exactly what I
meant. Or like this or that, (moves his hands) or whatever. All
these useless hand gimmicks.

Most of the people I know live on this fragile hope that—like
in the Truck Plant—that *They're going to definitely move in a
new vehicle there within the next year of two and I'll have a year
off just to lay back, soak up some unemployment and SUB-pay
and then I'll get called back.*

They're quite naive, a lot of these guys. But maybe that's
what they choose to believe.

It's preferable to thinking: I'm all done now. I never went to
college, I don't have any other skill. And I'm going to go from $14
to $3.50 an hour.

So, probably, the blind optimism is preferable.

So many of them don't have options. And if I were to be laid
off tomorrow, I wouldn't have any options. Because I barely
limped through high school and I don't have any other skill really.

You write.

Yeah, but all I ever got printed is what I write about the plant. And
it's sort of a convenient little gimmick I have running.

I don't have that burning urge to write about sports or fashion or politics. I just like writing about the steering gear man, or,
We got drunk this one Saturday night and some buffoon pulled his
pants down and . . .

It's obvious I've milked a good gimmick here. Apparently,
there's not too many autoworkers who are writing or detailing,
putting down on paper what's going on in their lives.

And I fit that mold real nice for all these publications who
say, "We need a voice of the working man."

Like today, I got a phone call from this magazine I've never
heard of called *Across the Board* from New York, and they want to
have me do this article. And I tell 'em, Well, you know, I don't
know how much time I've got. Then there's the *Penthouse*
thing . . .

So you feel you've been put into this little corner?

Yeah, I'm the designated blue-collar rivethead/wordsmith. I like
doing it. But I don't like it . . . I'm a shoprat, I'm proud of it.

But it became too much for me last year and I think that's when I had the problem. I was off for seven months. I got this idea in my head that I had to come up with all this profound worker stuff because people were calling me.

I just . . . I'm not very goal oriented.

You're saying you're hot?

Yeah, it's only the novelty of it, though. Well, I think it's good, but it's also the novelty of it. The novelty. If this was sports and I was writing a pretty good sports column, I would only blend in with five thousand names.

And every time *Sports Illustrated* wanted someone, they wouldn't come to the one certain guy: Well, this is the only guy that can really tell the story.

But it's been more like that with me: Well, we need this rivethead character to explain to us the ins-and-outs of the daily toil and stupid reminiscences of the lineworker.

I'm not trying to really bitch about it, but you get so many of these phone calls. It's all along the same level.

They're not saying it, but you can almost read . . . "You know, we always considered you shoprats were such dumb shits and here you are, you have half a brain and so we'd like to tap into it." They don't say that, but that's exactly it.

"We were so surprised to see that someone who writes as well as you do . . ." I mean, there's only what? Three hundred thousand shoprats in America, or whatever. And I'm sure I'm not the only one that can write. Or that the guy next to me isn't the only one that can water ski or the guy on the other side of me isn't the only guy that could build ships.

A lot of people, it's the only way they'll be spurred on to trying anything else is being faced with the absolute dilemma of not having a job.

Now, that way it might be good, because the talents that they've held in reserve might come to the forefront then.

But others are victims of their ancestry, off the feeder chain of ninety years of building cars or whatever and that's all they've ever prepared for.

And I think I've come from that stock. 'Cause both my grandfathers worked for GM and my grandmother and my dad. And really, I never . . . even in high school I knew I was going to be a shoprat. So I never tried to excel in anything because I knew it didn't make a damn bit of difference if I knew any geometry or if I knew past participles or if I knew whatever.

Yeah, just to screw a screw or to tip over a frame, or bolt some type of button.

I'm sure there are a lot of go-getters, but there's a lot of people who, if I was laid off yesterday or tomorrow, I'd be in their line.

Hell, I don't know, I was making $14 an hour acting like a shaved ape. I don't know what I'm going to do now. Except act like a shaved ape for $3.00 an hour.

How did you start writing?

Through sheer monotony and boredom and I guess an underlying friction in myself that just made me want to snap out at management and be sarcastic, sort of just be a tiny thorn in the side of General Motors.

It's such an all-encompassing empire that I thought if I could create this persona—I didn't sit down and map this out, but—I thought if I could create this persona and I was getting enough ink and enough being said about the mundane things which are really the actual things that keep General Motors moving every day. It's not Roger Smith showing off at some show.

But it was monotony. I had forty-five seconds between every job and I couldn't fill the damn thing up for five years, and I drank like a crazed man, which a lot of people do.

But I stumbled onto the writing. I'd work for forty-five seconds and then I finally turned it around to where I wrote for forty-five seconds. I'd just write down some abstract thing like *gray overalls* or something. But that would always come back to me. One sentence, or a quote somebody told me.

Later [I would] just assemble all this, and it would click back to me what *gray overalls* meant. Go through and sort of develop a story behind that.

And that's when time started passing faster for me on the line.

I can tell you exactly when my interest in literature started. I mean, I was just some goofball-asshole-D-student. But the nuns made us go down in eighth grade to the St. Luke's library, which was about as big as this corner [five square feet]. And they had a poetry section about this big [spreads his fingers one inch] and I said, Shit, these books are all thin. I'm going to take one of these. 'Cause they made you read them. And it was *Windsong* by Carl Sandburg. *Windsong*.

And I went home, and I was just bored and I'd read a few of these things, and I'd think, Goddamn, this shit don't even rhyme.

I kept reading: God, this one doesn't rhyme, either. And that's the first interest, right there, I ever got.

And then I really started voraciously reading. Wanting this kind of shit. I'd go to the library and take out anything. 'Cause I had always assumed before that point, that poetry was *Yes, the sky is sunny. I feel bright tonight.* Rhymed stuff.

Also, I really owe a heck of a debt to Mike Moore and the *Flint Voice,* because I'd just written some record reviews and he knew I was a factory worker and he liked my writing style through the record reviews.

And he said, "Why don't you try just vocalizing in the way you do your passions toward music, your passion toward your job or non-passion toward your job?" My angst or whatever.

I said, Well, Hell, I'd give it a try.

I said, "Who wants to hear about the steering gear man?"

He said, "You'd be surprised who wants to hear about the steering gear man."

I wrote four paragraphs about the steering gear man.

I think he got off on my fantasies about bowling with Roger Smith, which were obviously tongue-in-cheek but not as tongue-in-cheek as people seemed to believe.

I thought it would be the monster media show of the year if we could get me or Hogjaw to bowl with Roger Smith, have that on the network news.

Usually, everybody gets at least half a chance. You talk to your boss—Christmas party, a picnic, some damn thing. You get called on the carpet. Roger Smith is my actual boss even though I have ten thousand higher-ups that I have to answer to, but actually, he is my boss.

And you shouldn't have to bowl with everyone that works for GM. But as far as I can figure, I'm probably the first guy that asked, at least politely, at first.

I wonder if I'll be able to keep it [writing] up though, just in the little time that I've been at Pontiac—this place reminds me of the Stepford Wives.

God, it's just such a sterile environment. The floors actually shine and no one raises a voice.

And there's nothing interesting going on?

Well, I imagine there is, but I haven't put my finger on it yet. It used to be that every day on the rivet line was an event. It was just mayhem down there. Just mayhem. Who passed out on their job, who chopped off a finger, who put a rat in the foreman's salad or whatever.

Everybody's so goddamn serious about their work in Pontiac.

How long were you at the other place?

Nine and a half years. Truck and Bus.

You know what you might do. Call somebody up and say, "I'd like to try writing about this." And see what happens.

I've had offers, but I just . . . I also have a very low self-image. I'm really lethargic.

When did you start calling yourself a . . .

Rivethead?

. . . shoprat. Was it because of your family being in that area?

Yeah, they were shoprats. Anybody that works in the shop is a shoprat. Some people that work there don't like the term but that's . . . tough shit. They're a shoprat. I don't think that's a negative term.

How could you call anything, any job where you made four hundred bucks a week . . . You could call me *chief dick-sucker* (laughs) . . . If you're going to give me four hundred bucks a week call me *chief dick-sucker . . . shoprat*.

By the way, you were . . . not to change this . . . but you were talking about how you didn't have a lot of self-esteem.

Still don't.

Even on the best days on the rivet line, which were my favorite days, I never felt I had much in common with these guys outside of a hatred of authority and a love for alcohol. (Laughs.) But that's all we needed.

'Cause these guys were all into *I've got four snowmobiles; I've got a Lawnboy that has an atomic bag on it.*

And I don't even know what size car engine I drive. I don't know how to change the oil in my car and I just sit there and nod, but I'd take the conversation and run with it. After I'd had a few cold ones. And the stuff I knew I said, well, Jesus Christ, don't you remember [the song] "Psychotic Reaction" by The Count Five?

It's like: The Land Time Forgot—General Motors. I see people now that I hired in with ten and a half years ago and we were only just about drinking age, twenty and twenty-one. And now these are family men with three kids. And it's hard for me to realize or even recognize the fact that they've now got crows' feet and they're losing hair. Because we all still act like we're in tot lot.

GM is an extended adolescence. And when you were twenty-one and when you're thirty-one, it doesn't matter a lot.

I've got friends that I drink with sometimes and we'll go out and have a cold one at lunch who are forty-one, and I just don't think you'd see that kind of behavior with different groups of people at that age.

At General Motors, time really means nothing. It just goes by so quickly.

Oh, you're twenty-one. . . . Yeah, that's right and you were just the starting quarterback at Ferris State and now, shit you got two kids and stuff, you got two snowmobiles, you're losing all your hair and you've gained fifty pounds. But to me, you're the same wonderful guy. Let's have a couple Strohs.

I spent my last seven months not going out. Matter of fact, I'm on all kinds of medication now. I had to go to the Mental Health Clinic and stuff.

I wasn't out of it. I just couldn't handle working at the plant anymore. The walls started sweating and the ceiling started dripping, and Christ, I needed room to breathe. I had to get out of there. I had a series of panic attacks. To someone who hasn't had them I can't quite describe them.

If I were you and people said to me, "You're the voice of the working man," or act like that's the only thing you can write about, I guess that would bug me.

To me, it's like the white basketball player joke. Oh, a white guy who plays basketball. A shoprat who thinks, writes.

"You're the next Studs Terkel." It's like . . . *Penthouse* called me. At first I wasn't home. They called and told my wife. She said, Oh, yeah, *Penthouse* called for you, they want you to write an article. And I thought, What in the hell would *Penthouse* want me to . . .

So they called the next day and sure enough, it's "Well, we're doing this series on erotic adventures of . . . lifestyles . . . different jobs and shit . . . and we did the disc jockey that was having sex all night long with members of his audience . . . we did the insurance agent or whatever, the pool guard."

He says, "We want to hear about sex on the line." Christ, I don't know what to tell you, man. I've worked seven years on the rivet line. We never saw a woman. When we did we turned into a bunch of howling wolves, you know. *Owooo.* Screaming.

I mean, there were rumors that women worked there, but we worked in such a fucking low-life pit . . .

He said, "You could use a pseudonym, you know . . . If you're afraid of telling the real story." Hah! And I go, There is no real story. I mean, I could fabricate some kind of, "Well, then I bent her over the half-built Blazer . . ." (Laughs.)

I made attempts in the past, because I can write about music and I know about music. I filled out an application. Last summer when I was thinking I wasn't going to return to GM. I even talked to Al Peloquin [former editor of *Flint Journal*] himself. Went up to Big Al's office.

He's going, "Ben, I like your style, I've read your stuff." He goes, "However, we have a stack this high of college-educated people, you know." And I'm thinking, What? Just 'cause I didn't go to college? He goes, "Well, we have to take this into consideration."

I said, "Well, how many of these college-educated people have been named *Esquire* Man of the Year and been on the "Today Show" and been on the cover of *Mother Jones*," and you know, blah, toot-toot my own horn and all that shit, but.

I think there are a lot of things you could do anyway. If you're getting calls for "line porn," is that it?

Hey, I'd do it but I don't have the time right now. It's the total injustice. I was off for seven months and the phone didn't ring. As soon as I went back to work the *Free Press* is calling me, *Penthouse, Across the Board.*

I sort of have an ongoing relationship with the *Free Press.* I've been on the [Sunday magazine supplement] cover four times, written about eight stories altogether. I got a cover story coming up, should be early February. I gave it to them about two weeks ago. It's about my year off there.

When I was on the cover of *Mother Jones* a year and a half ago, they had this big media blitz tour planned for me and I went out on sick leave in August '86 and we hit all these towns, hit everywhere in Michigan.

And then I had to fly to Chicago by myself. I'd never been in an airplane and [my wife] Moira couldn't go with me. My nerves were too bad. I said, Hey, fuck this, hey, I ain't going. I had a 6:00 TV show in the morning.

And so I finally talked *Mother Jones* into letting a fellow linemate of mine, Dave, who's also in our band, the Shop Opera . . . they paid for his trip to go there.

It was like out of Fear and Loathing in Las Vegas. Goddamn. We stayed up all night and just got fucking drunk and shit. Then I went on to the show at six in the morning. This guy's interviewing me and I'm saying stuff like . . . They had this stupid-gimmick-bullshit thing . . . I don't know if you saw it in the *Journal* that one week about "You can read Ben Hamper in every issue of *Mother Jones*," and it said something about "He's been called the blue-collar Mike Royko," which I though was really funny.

So when I went to Chicago I went on this show and everyone referred to Mike Royko as a white-collar Ben Hamper. (Laughs.) These people were just cracking up.

We got out of there and I said, "Let's find out where this newspaper is that he writes for." And I couldn't remember if it was the *Tribune* or the *Sun-Times*. Here it is eight in the morning and we hadn't been to bed in forty-eight hours. We're drunk.

And we went to the wrong paper. And there's this big, black security guard, "Can I help you?" And we're obviously drunk on our asses. I go, "Yes, I'd like to see Mike Royko."

He said, "He doesn't work here. And beside the point, you look a little inebriated."

We were going to go out to Mike Royko's and say, "We hear you're the white-collar Ben Hamper." It was just so funny.

I can relate to you another story here. When we did that "Today Show" piece. They filmed it at Mark's Bar after work. And I had ten or fifteen linemates come over and we were all sitting there nursing Budweisers and all of a sudden, the producer says, "This is all on NBC. So go ahead and order whatever you want."

Shit! Everybody at the table: "I'll have four Heinekens, eight shots of Cognac." Shit, we ran up like $300 worth of booze at this one table in like an hour and a half.

Anyway. But this one guy I recognized from the plant, but I don't know his name, was on the other side of the bar. And they're filming us and we're just trying to act natural, not mugging for the camera. Saying, Yeah, it was hot there today, or whatever.

And this guy stumbles over, right when they're filming. He is more polluted than any three of us put together. And he just stumbles right in front of the camera.

He's grabbing the producer right by the collar going, "Jheshus

Christ, I hope you fucking assholes aren't trying to make all shoprats out to be goddamned alcoholics."

And the producer's going, "Shut the lights down." And two or three of us told him, "No, no, it's all right." He says, "You fuckers making fun of us. It's like we're dhruhnk all the time." And he was just polluted. And here he was. Staggers right up.

It's a wonder that didn't show up. I thought that should've showed up. It would have been great.

People are sensitive about it.

I used to think that it was a gallant, noble trade being a shoprat. But it really isn't. It's just . . . really all it is is prostitution.

One thing that I've never written about. And I don't know, I guess I'm a little timid about it because I'd really have to be serious and I hate to be serious very much.

Is the lack of racism in the plant. I went to parochial schools all my life so I didn't see a lot of black people. And when I first hired in at the Truck Plant, I don't have any figures, but through the years, it seemed 50–50 black and white. And we all made the same wage. We all kicked the same amount of ass and drank the beer just as fast as the other guy. And I made so many black friends. And there was never any hint of . . . *God, this guy happens to be black.*

This guy that worked a press, Eddie, for three years. He was black. He's from Mississippi. And we used to go out to his car after work some nights.

And he'd drink Cognac. Right out of the bottle. And he got me going on that. We would just sit there. We'd get a little loaded and talk. And he would tell me stuff, like . . .

"There was a time in my life I could never expect to do this with a white man. I mean, just my upbringing. I never saw a white person that lived in Mississippi," he'd say.

I said, "I went to parochial school. I never saw you black guys, either. But here we are." We were both making the same amount of wages. Going through the same amount of grind and monotony. And all of a sudden, the shade, the hue, just became nonexistent.

There's more rampant sexism in the plant than there is racism.

Ten to one.

We never saw women down on the rivet line. And it was a good thing.

They'd try some out now and then but it just . . . this isn't any slur against women or anything but the work is just strenuous as hell there. I mean, there were men there that didn't cut it. There was a couple women, but . . .

I'll tell you one story. I worked for two years on the rivet line right next to a girl named Janice.

And me and her became tight as hell.

And we would go out and have drinks after work and sometimes at lunch time. She was—and I hate to use the phrase—"One of the guys," like that's superior. (Leans into the microphone.) So I won't use that, strike that from the record!

Anyway, it really hurt me to see after a few months the . . . I guess, natural male response.

I used to get this stuff when she wasn't around, we'd be at bars with just guys. "You've been in her drawers, haven't ya?" And we never even touched.

She was just a beautiful person. She enjoyed my humor and I enjoyed her kindness and humor. And we would go out. We would go out Friday night. We had a date every Friday night.

One A.M. when that line closed for the week, I would meet her in the parking lot. My car. I would have a six pack of Bud. And I would buy her a bottle of . . . oh, Christ, what'd she drink? . . . some kind of wine . . . Liebfermilch or something. And she'd just drink it out of the bottle.

And we would watch all the shoprats come out and she would pick out all the women and she would say what they're going to do tonight.

And I would pick out all the men. As they're flying by the car, I'm going, "He's going home to masturbate. . . . He's going to a poker party." And she'd be going, "She's going to worry about her Tupperware party Sunday," and "She's got a baby shower."

And that's the kind of relationship we had. We'd finish that liquor and we'd go out and have eggs and toast and call it a night.

But it just disturbed me when the guys would always say, "What're you getting off her?" "I guess you been through that." It was just so, you know, ugh.

And the more you rebuke it, the more you stress the fact that you know it was true. The more they go, "Yeah." So I go, "Yeah, yeah, we're getting it on. What the hell. You get it on with somebody. You want to get it on with her, you try it."

Then they'd stop.

I worked in the shop once. When I started working there I got asked, "Are you a liberated woman?" And I thought, No, I wish I was. And I said, "No, not really," kind of chagrined, and they said "Oh, you don't mess around, then." And they had a very different understanding of what liberated *was. Liberated to them meant you were sexually experienced with everybody.*

You know more about the shop than I thought, by that remark. The answer to the question *Are you a liberated woman?* in the shop would be your definition of just what happened.

I sighed and said, No, like it was a failing. And they took it . . .

Oh, she won't get it on. She won't put out for a good job.
So, you've seen line work?

Yeah. They were paranoid about bringing any cameras in there. You just kind of notice they take it away.

They wouldn't let the goddamn "Today Show" in there.

They wouldn't let the "Today Show" in there?

On their bulletin board, their neon-fucking-sign boards they got in there, they would not allow the fact that I was to appear on the "Today Show" the next day. It's got: Joe Blow caught a 15-inch bass—Congratulations; Barry Smith bowled a 275 last night, congratulations. Ben Hamper's going to be on the "Today Show" tomorrow. *We can't print that.* I said, "Why?" He said, "Well, this isn't directly related to your job."
I said, "Oh, what about these people with the fish and stuff?" They said, "Well, it comes from a higher-up, you know." Blah-blah. It's obvious why they wouldn't.
But I got the last word on that "Today Show" piece. They wouldn't let us in the plant, and I said, Fine. The producer's name is Chris Brown. And I said, "Chris, bring your men over. At 6:30 we go to lunch, bring 'em on over, I'll show you where the pick up truck is." I pointed it out before the shift started.
I said, "Be there with the lamps and the cameras." And we had about five coolers of beer and about twenty people just chugging beer. Right on the line.
And it went on TV just as that. We're on our lunch hour. This is what we do. Ha!
Mike Moore got in there with me, once.
The last night he was to spend in Flint before he went to Frisco to start at *Mother Jones.* And I thought that was really cool of Mike, 'cause he's a man of the Flint soil and his old man was a

shoprat. And really he is. I've always told him he was a shoprat at heart.

And he said, "You know what I want to do my last night in Flint?" I said, "What? What? I'll take the night off. What do you want to do?"

He goes, "I want to come onto the rivet line." I said, "You want to come in here and go to the rivets? On your last night in Flint?" He goes, "Yeah."

So we rendezvoused out in the parking lot. I told him, I said, "Don't wear your stupid sweaters or your fucking moccasins and shit. Wear just tennis shoes and a Tiger ball cap and jeans."

And sure enough, he did. He came in there for about an hour and I taught him how to operate my rivet gun.

I was just thinking how cool this was. The last night. And if Roger Smith only knew what was going on because he knows Moore.

Are you getting a lot of these *I'm moving to Houston* stories?

No.

Three or four years ago, *I'm moving to Houston.* I know a guy who did that. He ended up selling shoes for like $2.25 an hour with all these promises of oil rigs and whatever. $2.25 an hour.

I heard you were interviewed by the New York Times.

Yeah, he came over to the Hyatt. He goes, "Where is there to drink?" He's just such an average guy. He goes, "Where is there to drink?"

I go, "Well, hey, you could go down to Billy's, the Torch, there's Churchills." He said, "Well, what's quickest?" I go, "Probably Churchills."

We walked down there and it was like, Yuppie city, and I said, "Well, another block down there's Billy's. If not there, we'll go to the Torch."

We wound up at the Torch.

And he bought—he's sort of a good ol' boy—he's got a big beer belly.

And he just started punching those Buds. And I didn't think there was a guy who could match me, but we went one for one. And we ended up, we drank from five 'til about one in the morning. We ended up in the Hyatt, up in their lounge, listening to some disco music.

I thought, He's not going to remember any of this. He didn't take any notes. Or well, very briefly. Every once in a while he'd go (makes writing motions). I thought, He's not getting any of this shit.

But sure enough, he didn't have a tape player or nothing.

Because I remember thinking the next day, waking up, Christ, I got fucked up out of that. It was like every half hour, he'd write something down. And I'd think, God, he's not getting it. And I'd ramble on and have these great like four minute statements.

But it got in there, anyway. One line will trigger it.

He was the best guy I'd ever been interviewed by. I don't want to sound like no celeb, but I've talked to a lot of people.

I think it's going to get bad in Flint this summer [1987]. This summer. 'Cause they're eating that SUB benefits like four, five credits per week. That shit ain't lasting for nothing. Anybody got laid off from August, September on is going to be down on their luck, come this summer.

You're going to see some wild shit. You always do in Flint, but you're going to see some mean stuff.

I worked with two or three guys who are laid off now, who made no bones about it, no contentions. When they heard they were going to be laid off. I said, "What are you going to do?" They said, "We'll sell drugs." Just like it was, *I'm going to peddle shoes. I'm going to sell drugs. I've got a friend of a friend of a friend.* They're going to do some eight ball and this and that.

You're going to have half the population moving into that, and half the population needing it, and the middle class . . . So everybody's going to have to fight for their right to party.

Shit. Fisher Body. Thirty-five hundred at our plant. I still call it our plant, the Truck Plant, thirty-five hundred went out then. Staggering. Buick City.

Rumors. They live on that. Rumors. 'Til this day, if you walked in right this minute, to the Truck Plant, low seniority people that are still hanging onto a job at the Truck Plant, you ask them, "Well, what do you think you're going to be doing in a year?" *Well, they're going to move in the uh, S-2 Van, the S-V Conforto . . .* whatever it is . . . *the Jetson Mobile.* George Jetson's going to order three thousand space machines.

They think it's this never-ending umbilical cord, you know, that just floats around, attached to them and GM.

If GM had said, maybe five, six years ago, "We are going to lay X amount of people off permanently, they're never going to be hired back because we're downsizing our operation." And then had offered training or whatever. Do you think that would have helped?

I'd say the vast majority of people would not have believed them. I'd be in that majority. I don't know why I went to Pontiac.

I started weighing all the people that I knew who were going down there. The guitarist in our band was going down there, the repairman in our department was going down there.

As stupid as it sounds, it's almost like a grade school type of thing. *God, all the popular people are going down there. The cool people.* I swear to God, that's how it was.

I really respected Dave 'cause he was a good guitarist. Tony Royale had a good rapport with the women. I thought, Well, geez. No really, that's about what it was. And all these dip-shits stayed behind, who had less time than I do, are still working.

I'd still be working in Flint. I could be driving two minutes to my job instead of forty-five. And I could double up instead of busting my ass on this wire job in Pontiac.

They're still down there working, but some are just like me, spending two months in the Mental Health Clinic, the same one I was at. Royale's been off for six months.

Well, I panicked. I just thought so much of Dave, the guitar player. And Tony Royale, the womanizer. I thought, These guys couldn't be wrong, they got everything going for them. They both look like gods, one guy plays the guitar, one guy plays the broads real well.

I thought, We got it over these other boneheads, we'll go to Pontiac. It was the stupidest move I made.

I'd have damn good seniority here at the Truck Plant. I'd probably never get laid off. But they had told me at the time. One of the recruiters. One of the presidents of the union, Danny Douglas, personally told me. He says, "Well, listen. You want a job in '87, with your seniority, you better go to Pontiac. Because there ain't no jobs for you in '87 in Flint." This was in '86 I was told this.

Give me that dotted line. I've got to have some income. So they buffaloed us. And it led to a lot of this mental strife I've had. Panic attacks. Anxiety attacks. This 'n' that.

Anybody can say, "Well, that's really cool and convenient for you to freak out," you know, but until you've been through it . . .

I had a nervous breakdown on the rivetline. I started crying and I'd rather have been hung up naked in front of the universe than to have twenty of my buddies see me crying. And that, that wasted me for a long time.

And I went back. I cried in front of at least twenty guys that I knew, that I drank beer with, talked snowmobiles with or pretended to.

I did go back. I had to go back.

Sick leave at GM is set up in such a way that I can understand, you know, the discrepancies and people's beliefs of what goes on with sick leave. *I've worked three months and now my back hurts.*

There's probably sixty percent bullshit and forty percent legitimate. But I never spent a moment on sick leave in ten years until these panic attacks. And believe me, I wish I'd have broken my arm, my leg, my neck, concussion, anything.

'Cause when I had them damn things, nothing could settle me. I'd get drunk. That's all I could do for like, two weeks. I sat in my apartment and didn't go to work. And drank. I'd get up in the morning and drink. I'd just start guzzling beer. I was so afraid.

Of what?

That I had lost it. That I could not go into a building with no windows and do a tedious job every forty-five seconds. I just totally lost it.

I think it was brought upon by the fact that I knew I had to leave for Pontiac and I realized that I made a mistake. The day after I signed up for Pontiac I didn't want to go. Something in my blood told me I didn't want to go, but I just thought, Well, Dave's going, Tony's going.

It's a crap decision. "The decision of your life." "Ben Hamper. This is your life. What are you going to do?"

You're not going to have a job in a year, well, okay, it's over, at least I got a job. Well, fuck it, I would have had a job anyway. Let's not get into this stupid shit. I'll start breaking bottles.

Hoodwinked. Hoodwinked by a totally useless union. The union down there in Pontiac is just like some type of groveling puppet show. Oh, God. I haven't seen a committeeman.

I asked a guy in Pontiac, "Why don't you put a 78 on that job?" A 78 is: There's too much work on this job, comparatively speaking. He said, "What's a 78?" I said, "How long have you worked here?" "Nine years." I said, "You never heard of a 78?" I just kept my mouth shut.

I wouldn't want to be a union person, unless I liked dough-nuts.

All I've found in my experience with Pontiac is that they should change the logo. You know how they've got the union logo that shows all the hands together? It should show about four or five guys handcuffed with the motto underneath saying, "My hands are tied."

I've run into that. *This is plant policy. I'd like to help you but my hands are tied.*

I was extremely fortunate for nine years. Seven out of those nine years, I was able to double up jobs with the guy next to me which meant that we went either half hour on, half hour off, day on, day off, half day on, half day off. And that's what kept it lively for us. Because when you were working, you were kicking ass. When you weren't, you were drinking at the bar. You were at home watching a movie. You were reading the sports page.

This grinds GM the wrong way, they don't want to hear this, but. That's the way it is. The worker will find a way. If the worker looks at his chum's operation and says, I could do that plus what I'm doing now. Sure as hell, later downstream, they're going to mate.

Compiling the jobs into one job. Where one guy hangs out. It might just start as a half hour. But in my greatest years at GM in '86, '85, it was a half day on, a half day off. I was out of there every night at 8:30 and I'd go home and I'd do the writing stuff. That's when I was really prolific with the writing. Yet still bringing home a hell of a decent wage.

And I can see what Sarah Goodsmith in Flint would read this in the *Flint Journal* and saying, They're supposed to be working but they go out to bars when they're getting paid, and somebody else is punching them out. Well, what would they do? What would they do?

What would you do? I'm asking Josie Kearns, what would you do?

If you worked next to a person and you could do that person's job, their job, for two hours, but then they could do their job and yours for two hours, and there was a bar two hundred yards across the street, what would you do? Yes, you'd go. And these people who write letters to the *Journal* and say, This is why our cars are fucked up, this is why it's all a mess.

That is total bullshit because the guys that double up, that have escapist tendencies, are the ones who do one hundred percent workmanship because we know we're hung, we're hung if we screw up a job and then the foreman has to come down and says, Where's Hamper? because something is screwed up. And then they say, He's over at Mark's Lounge. Then that's the end of the gimmick.

We do great work. Great work. When the average guy with the forty-five seconds off got sleepy, got drunk, got lackadaisical and shipped shit. I just want to go on record saying that I'm sick of these retirees and the macho men of the Depression saying this. They're full of horsefeathers.

There's a lot of trickery and rerouting amongst the workers, but the bottom line is, the foreman isn't going to let you go if you're screwing up. Whether it's two or three guys on one job, bottom line, if you can tie together with the guy next to you and put out a quality job and as much as they want and one hundred percent attendance and your nut is in such-and-such bolt, they're not going to say a word to you.

To me that can only be construed as a beautiful working relationship.

As far as the Japanese go, I've got to believe we're doing as good a job. Maybe they're more aerobic, skinnier than us with our beer bellies. But.

I bet you, I don't know this for a fact, but I bet you in Japan, when they have a problem on the line, they shut the goddamn thing down. In Flint, Pontiac, Wisconsin, Oshawa, whatever, they don't. You know what I mean? They don't shut the damn line down.

See, I have a problem. This damn thing shouldn't go beyond this point. They say, Let the sucker run, we've got to get out 250. Quota. Quota. Quota. It's just such an ironic thing that quality starts with a Q too, because that's what they harp on.

But when you say, "Man, this can't go beyond this point or this whole truck is going to be fucked up." They say, "Let it go. Let it go. They'll get it out in back, they'll get it back in the graveyard." "But we could fix it here if you take thirty seconds, stop the line, let this guy bring the part down, or bend this thing down." No, no, no, no.

"Shit, we gotta get 255 out or it's my ass on the fucking carpet tomorrow morning, you know."

Until they get over that . . .

The solution is to monitor the button that shuts the line down. Not every time a worker wants to shut it down, but monitor the button and pay attention to it. Let's get it fixed, let's do it.

But my experience has been if you turn on a button, right then, you're a criminal. It doesn't matter how fucked-up the job is. How corroded, eroded a job is. Let it go. Next station. Catch it later. You add up the catch-it-laters and then you get this shit on the road. People buy a $15,000 vehicle and shit starts rambling around, then that's their catch-you-laters.

I can't relate to mass quality. I can't relate to it. I know what Ben Hamper does. Right now, he ties down blinker lights and puts in the four-wheel drive shaft, right now. Two years ago, for seven years, he put in rear wheel castings and spring hangers. But Ben Hamper did a goddamn good job. And he spent half the day at the bar.

I see what it takes out of every person, what it takes out of me every day. But it's a trade-off. It's prostitution. It's not glamorous. It's not noble. It's prostitution. You're whoring your time. I'm whoring my time every day.

There's no reason I should have had to go through twelve years of the American educational system. There's no fucking reason for it.

If plant life is your future, you should have had an automatic exemption from ever having to go to school.

It's hard for me to forget all the times I was made to make up bullshit homework assignments. I could have spent all those winters playing basketball and springs playing baseball and falls playing hockey and football.

I could have skipped from kindergarten to the rivet line and not missed a beat.

Josie Kearns was born and raised in Flint, Michigan, where she still lives. She is the director of the Visiting Writers Series at The University of Michigan–Flint. A free-lance journalist, she has written articles for the *Flint Journal* and reviews for the *Detroit Free Press*. She won a Creative Artist Award from the Michigan Council for the Arts in 1986, a Major Hopwood Award for Poetry in 1983, and a Minor Hopwood Award for Poetry in 1981 and 1982. Her poetry has been published in the anthologies *Contemporary Michigan Poetry: Poems from the Third Coast* and *Industrial Strength Poetry,* and *Greenfield Review, Kansas Quarterly, Passages North,* and *Crosscurrents. Life After the Line* is her first book.

The manuscript was prepared for publication by Laurel Brandt and Paulette Petrimoulx. The book was designed by Elizabeth Hanson. The typeface for the text is Trump Roman and the display is Trump Bold.

Manufactured in the United States of America.